CONTENTS

1 Introduction 1
2 Breakfast Bonanza 5
3 Hearty Lunches 37
4 Comforting Dinners 69
5 Savory Sides 99
6 Sweet Treats 127
7 Snacks and Appetizers 157
8 Refreshing Beverages 189
9 Cooking Tips and Techniques 217

ABOUT THE AUTHOR 222
APPENDIX 225

Y'all Come Fix You a Plate Cookbook

Y'all Come Fix You a Plate Cookbook

Lila Thompson

Copyright © 2024 by Lila Thompson

All rights reserved. No part of this book may be reproduced in any manner whatsoever without written permission except in the case of brief quotations embodied in critical articles and reviews.

First Printing, 2024

1

Introduction

Howdy, y'all! Welcome to "Y'all Come Fix You a Plate Cookbook," a heartfelt collection of recipes straight from the heart of a barefoot neighbor. This ain't your fancy, highfalutin cookbook filled with things you can't pronounce or find at your local grocery store. Nope, this is a down-home, stick-to-your-ribs kind of cookbook, packed with dishes that'll make you feel like you're sitting at Grandma's table. Whether you're a seasoned home cook or just starting out, these recipes are meant to be cooked, enjoyed, and shared with those you love. So, kick off your shoes, grab a sweet tea, and let's get cookin'!

Author's Note

Hey there, friend. I'm thrilled you picked up this cookbook. Writing it has been a journey through the flavors and memories of my life, and I can't wait to share it with you. My love for cooking started in my Granny's kitchen, where the air always smelled like biscuits, bacon, and something sweet in the oven. Those moments taught me that food is more than just sustenance; it's love, comfort, and connection.

This cookbook is my way of passing on that love. It's filled with recipes that have been tried and true in my family, dishes that bring people together and make 'em feel at home. From breakfast to beverages, each recipe comes with a story, a bit of history, and a whole lotta heart. So, even if you're an asshole (kidding... kinda), I hope these recipes bring a smile to your face and warmth to your kitchen.

How to Use This Cookbook

This cookbook is designed to be as easy to use as a well-worn skillet. Here's a quick guide to help you navigate through these pages:

1. **Chapters**: The book is divided into seven chapters, covering everything from breakfast to beverages. Each chapter starts with a little story to set the mood and get your taste buds ready.

2. **Recipe Template**: Each recipe follows a simple template. You'll find all the information you need at a glance:

    - *Recipe Name*: What you're making.
    - *Servings, Prep Time, Cook Time*: How much it'll make and how long it'll take.
    - *Ingredients*: Everything you'll need, listed clearly.
    - *Instructions*: Step-by-step directions to get you from start to finish.
    - *Nutritional Information*: For those keeping track.

- *Cooking Tips*: Handy hints to make the cooking process smoother.
- *Allergen Information*: Common allergens and potential substitutes.

3. **Stories and Tips**: Throughout the book, you'll find stories from my kitchen and tips to help you along the way. They're here to add a personal touch and make your cooking experience even richer.

So, take your time, enjoy the journey, and don't be afraid to make these recipes your own. Cooking is about love, laughter, and a little bit of mess. Now, let's get started and fix us a plate!

2

Breakfast Bonanza

There's something magical about breakfast time. It's when the world wakes up, and the kitchen fills with the smell of coffee, sizzling bacon, and fresh biscuits. Growing up, breakfast was always a special time in my family. It was when we gathered around the table, still bleary-eyed but full of anticipation for the day ahead. These recipes are a tribute to those mornings, filled with warmth, love, and the promise of a new day. So, let's dive into these breakfast delights that will make you want to jump out of bed and head straight to the kitchen.

| 6 | – BREAKFAST BONANZA

Southern Biscuits and Gravy

Servings: 6 | *Prep Time:* 15 mins | *Cook Time:* 20 mins
Ingredients:

- 2 cups all-purpose flour
- 1 tablespoon baking powder
- 1 teaspoon salt
- 6 tablespoons cold butter, cubed
- 3/4 cup milk
- 1 pound breakfast sausage
- 1/4 cup all-purpose flour
- 2 cups milk
- Salt and pepper to taste

Instructions:

1. Preheat oven to 425°F (220°C).
2. In a large bowl, whisk together 2 cups flour, baking powder, and salt. Cut in the butter until the mixture resembles coarse crumbs. Stir in 3/4 cup milk until just combined.
3. Turn the dough out onto a floured surface and knead gently. Pat into a 1-inch-thick round and cut out biscuits with a floured cutter. Place on a baking sheet and bake for 12-15 minutes or until golden brown.
4. Meanwhile, cook sausage in a large skillet over medium heat until browned. Sprinkle 1/4 cup flour over the sausage and stir to coat. Gradually whisk in 2 cups milk, and cook until thickened. Season with salt and pepper.
5. Split the biscuits and top with sausage gravy.

Nutritional Information:

- Calories: 450
- Protein: 12g
- Carbs: 35g
- Fat: 28g

Cooking Tips:

- For flakier biscuits, handle the dough as little as possible.
- Add a pinch of red pepper flakes to the gravy for a spicy kick.

Allergen Information:

- Contains dairy and gluten. Substitute milk with a non-dairy alternative and use gluten-free flour if needed.

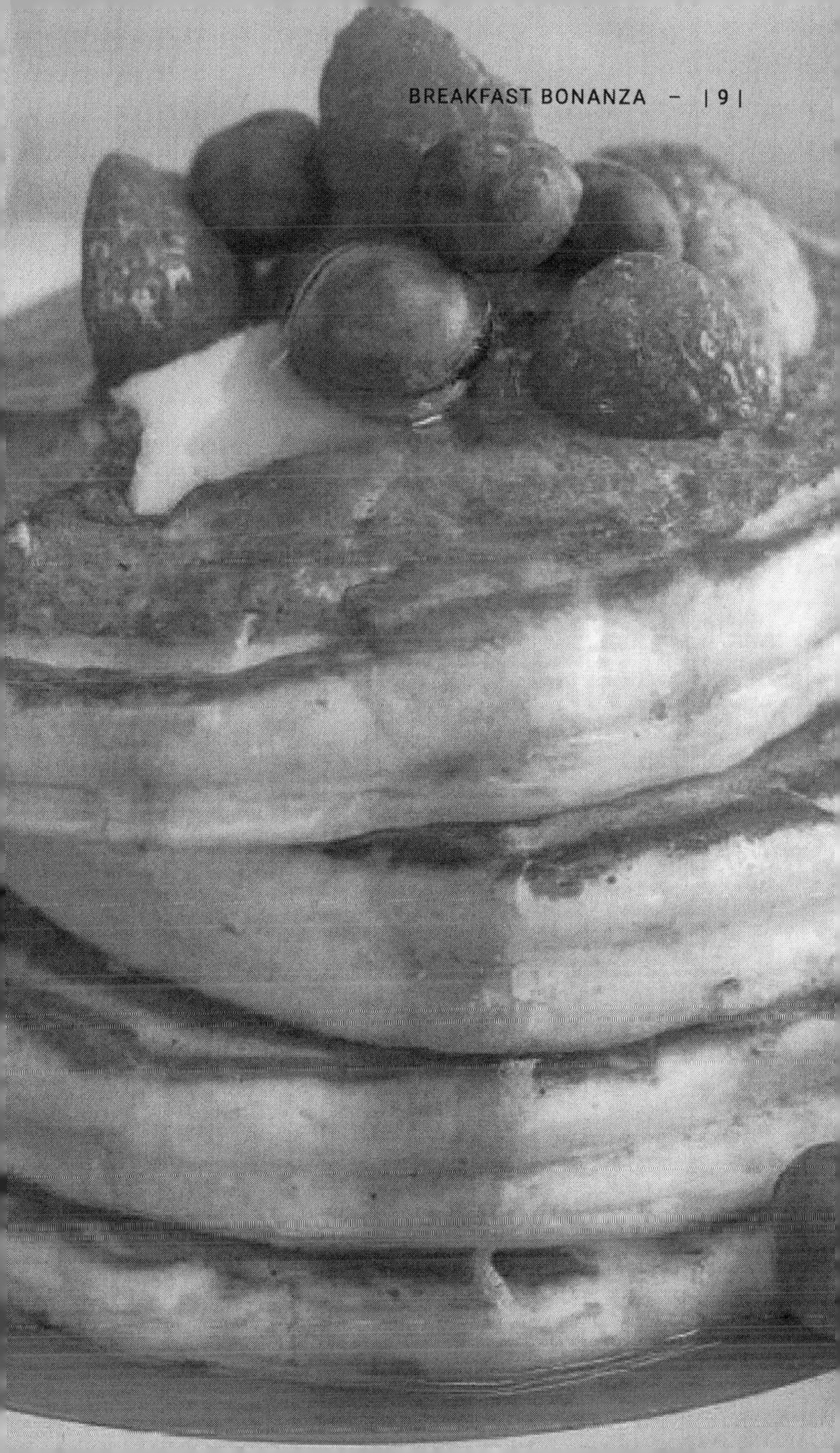

Fluffy Buttermilk Pancakes

Servings: 4 | *Prep Time:* 10 mins | *Cook Time:* 20 mins
Ingredients:

- 2 cups all-purpose flour
- 2 tablespoons sugar
- 2 teaspoons baking powder
- 1 teaspoon baking soda
- 1/2 teaspoon salt
- 2 cups buttermilk
- 2 large eggs
- 1/4 cup melted butter
- 1 teaspoon vanilla extract

Instructions:

1. In a large bowl, whisk together flour, sugar, baking powder, baking soda, and salt.
2. In another bowl, whisk together buttermilk, eggs, melted butter, and vanilla extract. Pour the wet ingredients into the dry ingredients and stir until just combined.
3. Heat a griddle or large skillet over medium heat and lightly grease with butter or oil. Pour 1/4 cup of batter onto the griddle for each pancake. Cook until bubbles form on the surface, then flip and cook until golden brown on the other side.
4. Serve hot with butter and syrup.

Nutritional Information:

- Calories: 320
- Protein: 8g
- Carbs: 45g
- Fat: 12g

Cooking Tips:

- Don't overmix the batter; lumps are okay.
- For extra flavor, add a handful of blueberries or chocolate chips to the batter.

Allergen Information:

- Contains dairy and eggs. Substitute buttermilk with a non-dairy alternative and use an egg replacer if needed.

| 12 | - BREAKFAST BONANZA

Classic Cheese Grits

Servings: 6 | *Prep Time:* 5 mins | *Cook Time:* 25 mins
Ingredients:

- 1 cup stone-ground grits
- 4 cups water
- 1 teaspoon salt
- 1 cup shredded sharp cheddar cheese
- 4 tablespoons butter
- 1/4 teaspoon black pepper

Instructions:

1. In a large saucepan, bring water to a boil. Add salt and slowly stir in the grits. Reduce heat to low and cook, stirring frequently, until the grits are thick and creamy, about 20-25 minutes.
2. Remove from heat and stir in cheese, butter, and black pepper until melted and smooth.
3. Serve hot, garnished with additional cheese if desired.

Nutritional Information:

- Calories: 240
- Protein: 7g
- Carbs: 29g
- Fat: 11g

Cooking Tips:

- Stir constantly to prevent grits from clumping or sticking.
- For a richer flavor, substitute half the water with milk or chicken broth.

Allergen Information:

- Contains dairy. Use a dairy-free cheese and butter alternative if needed.

BREAKFAST BONANZA - |15|

Country Ham and Eggs

Servings: 4 | *Prep Time:* 5 mins | *Cook Time:* 15 mins
Ingredients:

- 4 slices country ham
- 8 large eggs
- 2 tablespoons butter
- Salt and pepper to taste

Instructions:

1. Heat a large skillet over medium heat and add the ham slices. Cook until browned and heated through, about 3-4 minutes per side. Remove from the skillet and set aside.
2. In the same skillet, melt the butter over medium-low heat. Crack the eggs into the skillet and cook until the whites are set and the yolks are to your desired doneness.
3. Season with salt and pepper and serve immediately with the ham.

Nutritional Information:

- Calories: 300
- Protein: 25g
- Carbs: 1g
- Fat: 22g

Cooking Tips:

- For perfectly cooked eggs, use fresh eggs and cook them on low heat.
- Add a splash of water to the skillet and cover it to steam the eggs for a softer yolk.

Allergen Information:

- Contains eggs. Use an egg substitute if needed.

| 18 | - BREAKFAST BONANZA

Sweet Potato Hash Browns

Servings: 4 | *Prep Time:* 10 mins | *Cook Time:* 15 mins
Ingredients:

- 2 large sweet potatoes, peeled and grated
- 1 small onion, grated
- 1/4 cup all-purpose flour
- 1 large egg
- Salt and pepper to taste
- 1/4 cup vegetable oil

Instructions:

1. In a large bowl, combine the grated sweet potatoes, onion, flour, and egg. Season with salt and pepper and mix well.
2. Heat the vegetable oil in a large skillet over medium-high heat. Drop spoonfuls of the sweet potato mixture into the skillet and flatten with a spatula.
3. Cook until golden brown and crispy, about 3-4 minutes per side. Remove to a paper towel-lined plate to drain excess oil.
4. Serve hot, garnished with additional salt and pepper if desired.

Nutritional Information:

- Calories: 220
- Protein: 3g
- Carbs: 25g
- Fat: 12g

Cooking Tips:

- Squeeze out excess moisture from the grated sweet potatoes and onions for crispier hash browns.
- Add spices like paprika or garlic powder for extra flavor.

Allergen Information:

- Contains eggs and gluten. Use a gluten-free flour and egg substitute if needed.

BREAKFAST BONANZA — | 21 |

Banana Nut Muffins

Servings: 12 | *Prep Time:* 15 mins | *Cook Time:* 20 mins
Ingredients:

- 1 1/2 cups all-purpose flour
- 1 teaspoon baking soda
- 1/2 teaspoon salt
- 3 large ripe bananas, mashed
- 3/4 cup granulated sugar
- 1/3 cup melted butter
- 1 large egg
- 1 teaspoon vanilla extract
- 1/2 cup chopped walnuts

Instructions:

1. Preheat oven to 350°F (175°C) and line a muffin tin with paper liners.
2. In a medium bowl, whisk together flour, baking soda, and salt.
3. In a large bowl, mix together the mashed bananas, sugar, melted butter, egg, and vanilla extract. Gradually add the dry ingredients to the wet ingredients and stir until just combined. Fold in the chopped walnuts.
4. Divide the batter evenly among the muffin cups and bake for 18-20 minutes or until a toothpick inserted into the center comes out clean.
5. Let cool in the pan for 5 minutes before transferring to a wire rack to cool completely.

Nutritional Information:

- Calories: 200
- Protein: 4g
- Carbs: 30g
- Fat: 8g

Cooking Tips:

- For an extra moist muffin, use overripe bananas.
- Sprinkle additional chopped walnuts on top of the batter before baking for a crunchy topping.

Allergen Information:

- Contains gluten, dairy, eggs, and nuts. Use gluten-free flour, dairy-free butter, egg substitute, and omit nuts if needed.

| 24 | - BREAKFAST BONANZA

Homemade Granola with Fresh Fruit

Servings: 8 | *Prep Time:* 10 mins | *Cook Time:* 30 mins
Ingredients:

- 3 cups old-fashioned oats
- 1 cup sliced almonds
- 1/2 cup shredded coconut
- 1/2 cup honey
- 1/3 cup vegetable oil
- 1 teaspoon vanilla extract
- 1/2 teaspoon salt
- Fresh fruit (e.g., berries, bananas, apples), for serving

Instructions:

1. Preheat oven to 300°F (150°C) and line a baking sheet with parchment paper.
2. In a large bowl, combine oats, almonds, and coconut.
3. In a small saucepan, combine honey, vegetable oil, vanilla extract, and salt. Heat over medium heat until the mixture is smooth and combined. Pour over the oat mixture and stir until evenly coated.
4. Spread the granola mixture in an even layer on the prepared baking sheet. Bake for 25-30 minutes, stirring halfway through, until golden brown.
5. Let cool completely on the baking sheet before transferring to an airtight container.
6. Serve granola with fresh fruit and your favorite yogurt or milk.

Nutritional Information:

- Calories: 280
- Protein: 5g
- Carbs: 40g
- Fat: 12g

Cooking Tips:

- For a different flavor, substitute maple syrup for honey.
- Add dried fruits like raisins or cranberries after baking for added sweetness.

Allergen Information:

- Contains nuts. Omit or substitute with seeds if needed.

BREAKFAST BONANZA — | 27 |

Blueberry Scones

Servings: 8 | *Prep Time:* 15 mins | *Cook Time:* 20 mins
Ingredients:

- 2 cups all-purpose flour
- 1/4 cup granulated sugar
- 2 teaspoons baking powder
- 1/2 teaspoon salt
- 1/2 cup cold butter, cubed
- 1/2 cup heavy cream
- 1 large egg
- 1 teaspoon vanilla extract
- 1 cup fresh or frozen blueberries

Instructions:

1. Preheat oven to 400°F (200°C) and line a baking sheet with parchment paper.
2. In a large bowl, whisk together flour, sugar, baking powder, and salt. Cut in the cold butter until the mixture resembles coarse crumbs.
3. In a small bowl, whisk together heavy cream, egg, and vanilla extract. Add the wet ingredients to the dry ingredients and stir until just combined. Gently fold in the blueberries.
4. Turn the dough out onto a floured surface and shape into an 8-inch circle. Cut into 8 wedges and place on the prepared baking sheet.
5. Bake for 18-20 minutes or until golden brown. Let cool on a wire rack before serving.

Nutritional Information:

- Calories: 250
- Protein: 4g
- Carbs: 34g
- Fat: 11g

Cooking Tips:

- For extra sweetness, sprinkle the tops of the scones with coarse sugar before baking.
- If using frozen blueberries, do not thaw them before adding to the dough.

Allergen Information:

- Contains gluten, dairy, and eggs. Use gluten-free flour, dairy-free cream, and an egg substitute if needed.

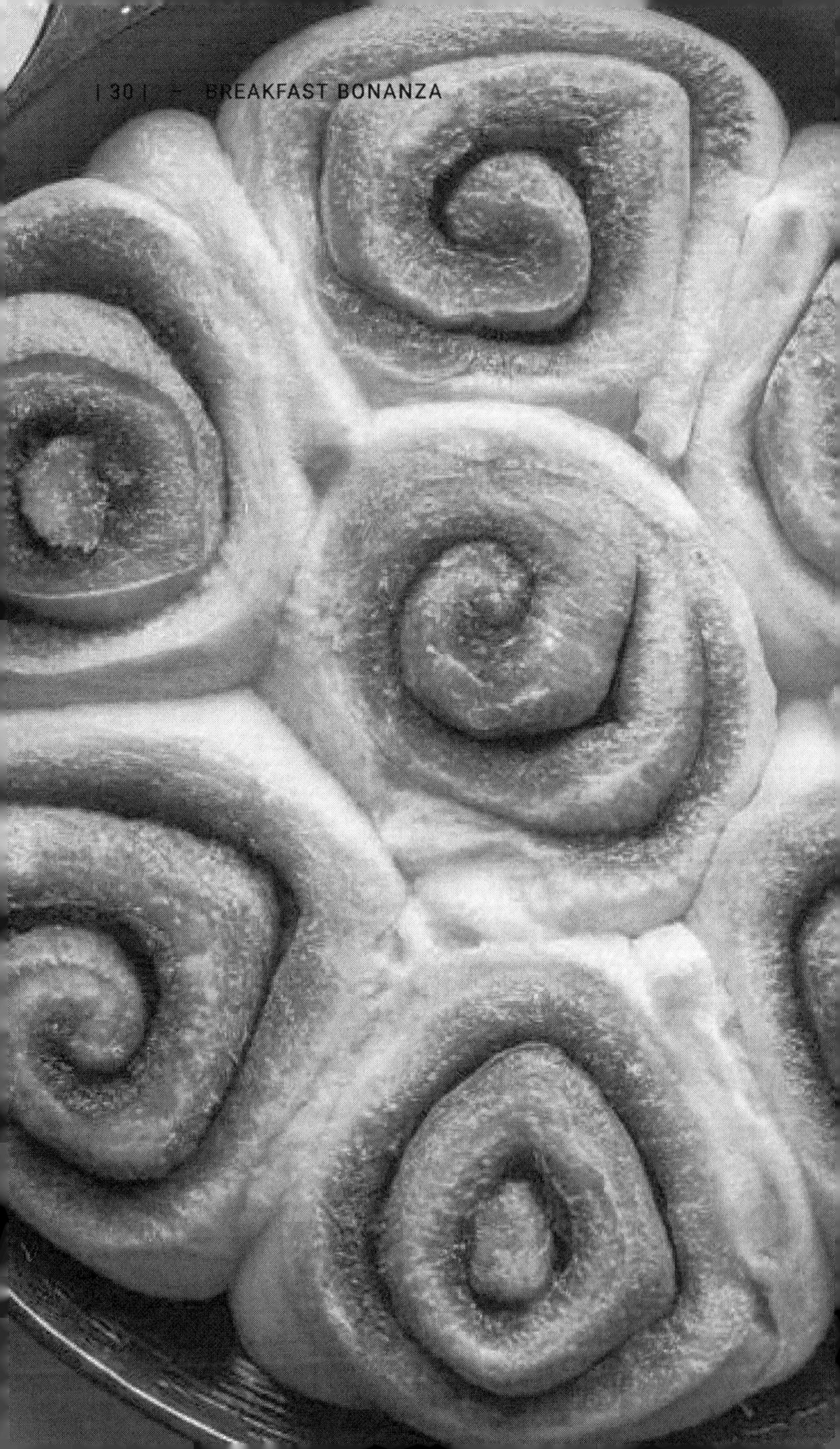

Cinnamon Rolls

Servings: 12 | *Prep Time:* 30 mins | *Cook Time:* 25 mins
Ingredients:

- 1 cup warm milk (110°F/45°C)
- 2 1/4 teaspoons active dry yeast
- 1/2 cup granulated sugar
- 1/3 cup melted butter
- 1 teaspoon salt
- 2 large eggs
- 4 cups all-purpose flour
- 1 cup packed brown sugar
- 2 1/2 tablespoons ground cinnamon
- 1/3 cup butter, softened
- 1/2 cup cream cheese, softened
- 1/4 cup butter, softened
- 1 1/2 cups powdered sugar
- 1/2 teaspoon vanilla extract
- 1/8 teaspoon salt

Instructions:

1. In a large bowl, dissolve yeast in warm milk. Add sugar, melted butter, salt, eggs, and flour. Mix well and knead the dough for about 5-7 minutes until smooth and elastic. Place in a greased bowl, cover, and let rise in a warm place until doubled in size, about 1 hour.
2. Roll the dough out on a lightly floured surface into a 16x21-inch rectangle. Spread softened butter over the dough.

Mix brown sugar and cinnamon and sprinkle over the buttered dough. Roll up the dough tightly and cut into 12 rolls.
3. Place rolls in a greased 9x13-inch baking dish. Cover and let rise until nearly doubled, about 30 minutes. Preheat oven to 375°F (190°C).
4. Bake rolls in preheated oven until golden brown, about 25 minutes. While the rolls are baking, make the frosting by beating together cream cheese, butter, powdered sugar, vanilla extract, and salt.
5. Spread frosting over warm rolls before serving.

Nutritional Information:

- Calories: 450
- Protein: 6g
- Carbs: 72g
- Fat: 17g

Cooking Tips:

- For gooey cinnamon rolls, pour a little heavy cream over the rolls before baking.
- Add chopped nuts or raisins to the filling for added texture and flavor.

Allergen Information:

- Contains gluten, dairy, and eggs. Use gluten-free flour, dairy-free butter and cream cheese, and an egg substitute if needed.

BREAKFAST BONANZA — |33|

Breakfast Casserole

Servings: 8 | *Prep Time:* 15 mins | *Cook Time:* 45 mins
Ingredients:

- 1 pound breakfast sausage
- 6 slices bread, cubed
- 2 cups shredded cheddar cheese
- 6 large eggs
- 2 cups milk
- 1 teaspoon mustard powder
- Salt and pepper to taste

Instructions:

1. Preheat oven to 350°F (175°C) and grease a 9x13-inch baking dish.
2. In a large skillet, cook sausage over medium heat until browned and crumbled. Drain any excess fat.
3. Spread the bread cubes in the prepared baking dish. Sprinkle the cooked sausage and shredded cheese evenly over the bread.
4. In a large bowl, whisk together eggs, milk, mustard powder, salt, and pepper. Pour the egg mixture over the bread, sausage, and cheese.
5. Bake in preheated oven until the top is golden and the casserole is set, about 45 minutes. Let cool for 5-10 minutes before serving.

Nutritional Information:

- Calories: 350
- Protein: 18g
- Carbs: 18g
- Fat: 24g

Cooking Tips:

- Prepare the casserole the night before and refrigerate overnight for a quick and easy breakfast.
- Add vegetables like bell peppers, onions, or spinach for extra flavor and nutrition.

Allergen Information:

- Contains gluten, dairy, and eggs. Use gluten-free bread, dairy-free cheese and milk, and an egg substitute if needed.

3

Hearty Lunches

Lunchtime in the South is more than just a break in the middle of the day; it's a time to gather, share stories, and enjoy comforting food that keeps you going. Family lunches are often filled with laughter, the clinking of glasses, and the aroma of something delicious wafting from the kitchen. These hearty lunch recipes are designed to bring that sense of community and warmth to your table. From satisfying sandwiches to rich, flavorful soups, these dishes will make your mid-day meal something to look forward to. So, let's dive into these Southern classics that are sure to become lunchtime favorites.

| 38 | - HEARTY LUNCHES

Fried Chicken Sandwich

Servings: 4 | *Prep Time:* 20 mins | *Cook Time:* 15 mins
Ingredients:

- 4 boneless, skinless chicken breasts
- 1 cup buttermilk
- 1 cup all-purpose flour
- 1 teaspoon paprika
- 1 teaspoon garlic powder
- 1/2 teaspoon salt
- 1/2 teaspoon black pepper
- 1 cup vegetable oil, for frying
- 4 hamburger buns
- Lettuce, tomato, and pickles, for serving
- Mayonnaise, for serving

Instructions:

1. Place chicken breasts between two pieces of plastic wrap and pound to an even thickness.
2. In a bowl, combine buttermilk, paprika, garlic powder, salt, and pepper. Add chicken breasts, cover, and refrigerate for at least 1 hour.
3. In a shallow dish, place the flour. Dredge each chicken breast in the flour, coating completely.
4. Heat vegetable oil in a large skillet over medium-high heat. Fry the chicken breasts until golden brown and cooked through, about 5-7 minutes per side. Remove and drain on paper towels.

5. Toast the hamburger buns in the skillet until golden. Assemble the sandwiches with fried chicken, lettuce, tomato, pickles, and mayonnaise.

Nutritional Information:

- Calories: 600
- Protein: 35g
- Carbs: 50g
- Fat: 30g

Cooking Tips:

- For extra crispy chicken, double-dip in buttermilk and flour.
- Add a splash of hot sauce to the buttermilk marinade for a spicy kick.

Allergen Information:

- Contains gluten and dairy. Use gluten-free flour and a dairy-free buttermilk alternative if needed.

HEARTY LUNCHES — |41|

Tomato Basil Soup

Servings: 6 | *Prep Time:* 10 mins | *Cook Time:* 30 mins
Ingredients:

- 2 tablespoons olive oil
- 1 onion, chopped
- 3 cloves garlic, minced
- 2 (28-ounce) cans crushed tomatoes
- 2 cups chicken or vegetable broth
- 1/4 cup chopped fresh basil
- 1 tablespoon sugar
- Salt and pepper to taste
- 1/2 cup heavy cream (optional)

Instructions:

1. In a large pot, heat olive oil over medium heat. Add onion and garlic, and cook until softened, about 5 minutes.
2. Stir in the crushed tomatoes and broth. Bring to a simmer and cook for 20 minutes.
3. Add the chopped basil and sugar. Season with salt and pepper. For a creamy soup, stir in the heavy cream and heat through.
4. Use an immersion blender to puree the soup until smooth. Alternatively, carefully transfer the soup to a blender in batches.
5. Serve hot, garnished with fresh basil leaves.

Nutritional Information:

- Calories: 180
- Protein: 3g
- Carbs: 20g
- Fat: 10g

Cooking Tips:

- For a richer flavor, roast the tomatoes and garlic before adding them to the soup.
- Serve with a grilled cheese sandwich for a classic combination.

Allergen Information:

- Contains dairy (optional). Use a non-dairy cream substitute if needed.

| 44 | - HEARTY LUNCHES

Pulled Pork Sliders

Servings: 8 | *Prep Time:* 15 mins | *Cook Time:* 6 hours (slow cooker)

Ingredients:

- 2 pounds pork shoulder
- 1 tablespoon paprika
- 1 tablespoon brown sugar
- 1 teaspoon garlic powder
- 1 teaspoon onion powder
- 1 teaspoon salt
- 1/2 teaspoon black pepper
- 1/2 teaspoon cayenne pepper
- 1 cup BBQ sauce
- 16 slider buns
- Coleslaw, for serving

Instructions:

1. In a small bowl, combine paprika, brown sugar, garlic powder, onion powder, salt, black pepper, and cayenne pepper. Rub the spice mixture all over the pork shoulder.
2. Place the pork shoulder in a slow cooker and cook on low for 6-8 hours, or until the meat is tender and easily shredded with a fork.
3. Remove the pork from the slow cooker and shred with two forks. Stir in the BBQ sauce.
4. Serve the pulled pork on slider buns, topped with coleslaw.

Nutritional Information:

- Calories: 300
- Protein: 20g
- Carbs: 30g
- Fat: 10g

Cooking Tips:

- For extra flavor, sear the pork shoulder in a hot skillet before placing it in the slow cooker.
- Use the leftover pulled pork for sandwiches, tacos, or nachos.

Allergen Information:

- Contains gluten. Use gluten-free buns if needed.

HEARTY LUNCHES — | 47 |

Southern Cobb Salad

Servings: 4 | *Prep Time:* 20 mins | *Cook Time:* 10 mins
Ingredients:

- 6 cups mixed greens
- 2 grilled chicken breasts, sliced
- 4 hard-boiled eggs, quartered
- 1 avocado, sliced
- 1 cup cherry tomatoes, halved
- 1/2 cup blue cheese crumbles
- 6 slices bacon, cooked and crumbled
- 1/2 cup ranch dressing

Instructions:

1. On a large platter, arrange the mixed greens.
2. Top with grilled chicken, hard-boiled eggs, avocado, cherry tomatoes, blue cheese crumbles, and bacon.
3. Drizzle with ranch dressing and serve immediately.

Nutritional Information:

- Calories: 500
- Protein: 35g
- Carbs: 12g
- Fat: 36g

Cooking Tips:

- For a lighter dressing, mix equal parts ranch dressing and Greek yogurt.
- Add other favorite toppings like cucumbers, red onions, or olives.

Allergen Information:

- Contains dairy and eggs. Use a dairy-free dressing and egg substitute if needed.

| 50 | — HEARTY LUNCHES

Pimento Cheese Spread

Servings: 8 | *Prep Time:* 10 mins | *Cook Time:* 0 mins
Ingredients:

- 2 cups shredded sharp cheddar cheese
- 1/2 cup mayonnaise
- 1 (4-ounce) jar diced pimentos, drained
- 1/4 teaspoon garlic powder
- 1/4 teaspoon onion powder
- Salt and pepper to taste

Instructions:

1. In a large bowl, combine shredded cheddar cheese, mayonnaise, diced pimentos, garlic powder, onion powder, salt, and pepper. Mix until well combined.
2. Serve immediately with crackers, bread, or vegetables, or refrigerate until ready to use.

Nutritional Information:

- Calories: 200
- Protein: 8g
- Carbs: 2g
- Fat: 18g

Cooking Tips:

- For a spicier spread, add a dash of hot sauce or cayenne pepper.
- Use as a filling for sandwiches or as a topping for burgers.

Allergen Information:

- Contains dairy and eggs. Use dairy-free cheese and mayonnaise if needed.

HEARTY LUNCHES — | 53 |

Shrimp and Grits

Servings: 4 | *Prep Time:* 15 mins | *Cook Time:* 25 mins
Ingredients:

- 1 cup stone-ground grits
- 4 cups water
- 1 teaspoon salt
- 1 cup shredded sharp cheddar cheese
- 4 tablespoons butter
- 1/4 teaspoon black pepper
- 1 pound large shrimp, peeled and deveined
- 4 slices bacon, chopped
- 1 small onion, chopped
- 1 bell pepper, chopped
- 2 cloves garlic, minced
- 1/2 cup chicken broth
- 1 tablespoon lemon juice
- 1 tablespoon chopped fresh parsley

Instructions:

1. In a large saucepan, bring water to a boil. Add salt and slowly stir in the grits. Reduce heat to low and cook, stirring frequently, until the grits are thick and creamy, about 20-25 minutes. Stir in cheese, butter, and black pepper.
2. In a large skillet, cook bacon over medium heat until crispy. Remove bacon and set aside, leaving the drippings in the skillet.

3. Add shrimp to the skillet and cook until pink, about 2-3 minutes per side. Remove shrimp and set aside.
4. In the same skillet, add onion and bell pepper and cook until softened, about 5 minutes. Add garlic and cook for another minute.
5. Stir in chicken broth and lemon juice, scraping up any browned bits from the bottom of the skillet. Return shrimp and bacon to the skillet and cook until heated through.
6. Serve shrimp mixture over the cheese grits, garnished with fresh parsley.

Nutritional Information:

- Calories: 450
- Protein: 30g
- Carbs: 35g
- Fat: 20g

Cooking Tips:

- For creamier grits, substitute half the water with milk or chicken broth.
- Add a pinch of cayenne pepper for a bit of heat.

Allergen Information:

- Contains dairy and shellfish. Use dairy-free cheese and butter if needed.

| 56 | - HEARTY LUNCHES

Chicken Salad Wraps

Servings: 4 | *Prep Time:* 15 mins | *Cook Time:* 0 mins
Ingredients:

- 2 cups cooked, shredded chicken
- 1/2 cup mayonnaise
- 1/4 cup chopped celery
- 1/4 cup chopped red onion
- 1/4 cup chopped pecans
- 1 tablespoon lemon juice
- Salt and pepper to taste
- 4 large lettuce leaves or tortilla wraps
- Sliced avocado, for serving (optional)

Instructions:

1. In a large bowl, combine shredded chicken, mayonnaise, celery, red onion, pecans, lemon juice, salt, and pepper. Mix until well combined.
2. Spoon the chicken salad onto lettuce leaves or tortilla wraps. Add sliced avocado if desired.
3. Roll up and serve immediately.

Nutritional Information:

- Calories: 300
- Protein: 20g
- Carbs: 8g
- Fat: 22g

Cooking Tips:

- For a lighter version, use Greek yogurt instead of mayonnaise.
- Add dried cranberries or grapes for a touch of sweetness.

Allergen Information:

- Contains nuts and eggs. Omit nuts and use an egg-free mayonnaise if needed.

HEARTY LUNCHES — |59|

Vegetable Quiche

Servings: 6 | Prep Time: 15 mins | Cook Time: 45 mins
Ingredients:

- 1 pie crust (store-bought or homemade)
- 1 tablespoon olive oil
- 1 small onion, chopped
- 1 bell pepper, chopped
- 1 zucchini, chopped
- 1 cup chopped spinach
- 1 cup shredded cheese (cheddar, Swiss, or a mix)
- 4 large eggs
- 1 cup milk
- Salt and pepper to taste

Instructions:

1. Preheat oven to 375°F (190°C). Place the pie crust in a 9-inch pie dish and set aside.
2. In a large skillet, heat olive oil over medium heat. Add onion, bell pepper, and zucchini, and cook until softened, about 5 minutes. Stir in the spinach and cook until wilted. Remove from heat and let cool slightly.
3. Spread the cooked vegetables in the pie crust. Sprinkle the shredded cheese over the vegetables.
4. In a large bowl, whisk together eggs, milk, salt, and pepper. Pour the egg mixture over the vegetables and cheese.

5. Bake for 35-45 minutes, or until the quiche is set and the top is golden brown. Let cool for 10 minutes before slicing and serving.

Nutritional Information:

- Calories: 300
- Protein: 12g
- Carbs: 22g
- Fat: 20g

Cooking Tips:

- For a richer quiche, use half-and-half instead of milk.
- Add other favorite vegetables or cooked bacon for extra flavor.

Allergen Information:

- Contains dairy, eggs, and gluten. Use a gluten-free crust, dairy-free cheese, and milk if needed.

| 62 | - HEARTY LUNCHES

Chicken Pot Pie

Servings: 6 | *Prep Time:* 20 mins | *Cook Time:* 40 mins
Ingredients:

- 1 pie crust (store-bought or homemade)
- 1/3 cup butter
- 1/3 cup all-purpose flour
- 1/2 teaspoon salt
- 1/4 teaspoon black pepper
- 1/4 teaspoon onion powder
- 1/4 teaspoon garlic powder
- 1/4 teaspoon dried thyme
- 1 3/4 cups chicken broth
- 2/3 cup milk
- 3 cups cooked, shredded chicken
- 1 cup frozen peas and carrots, thawed

Instructions:

1. Preheat oven to 425°F (220°C). Place the pie crust in a 9-inch pie dish and set aside.
2. In a large saucepan, melt butter over medium heat. Stir in flour, salt, pepper, onion powder, garlic powder, and thyme until well combined and bubbly.
3. Gradually whisk in chicken broth and milk. Cook, stirring constantly, until the mixture is thickened and bubbly.
4. Stir in shredded chicken and peas and carrots. Remove from heat and let cool slightly.

5. Pour the chicken mixture into the pie crust. Roll out the second pie crust and place it over the filling. Trim and seal the edges, and cut slits in the top crust to allow steam to escape.
6. Bake for 30-40 minutes, or until the crust is golden brown and the filling is bubbly. Let cool for 10 minutes before serving.

Nutritional Information:

- Calories: 400
- Protein: 25g
- Carbs: 30g
- Fat: 20g

Cooking Tips:

- For a shortcut, use rotisserie chicken and store-bought pie crust.
- Add other vegetables like mushrooms, corn, or green beans for extra nutrition.

Allergen Information:

- Contains gluten and dairy. Use a gluten-free crust and dairy-free butter and milk if needed.

HEARTY LUNCHES | 65

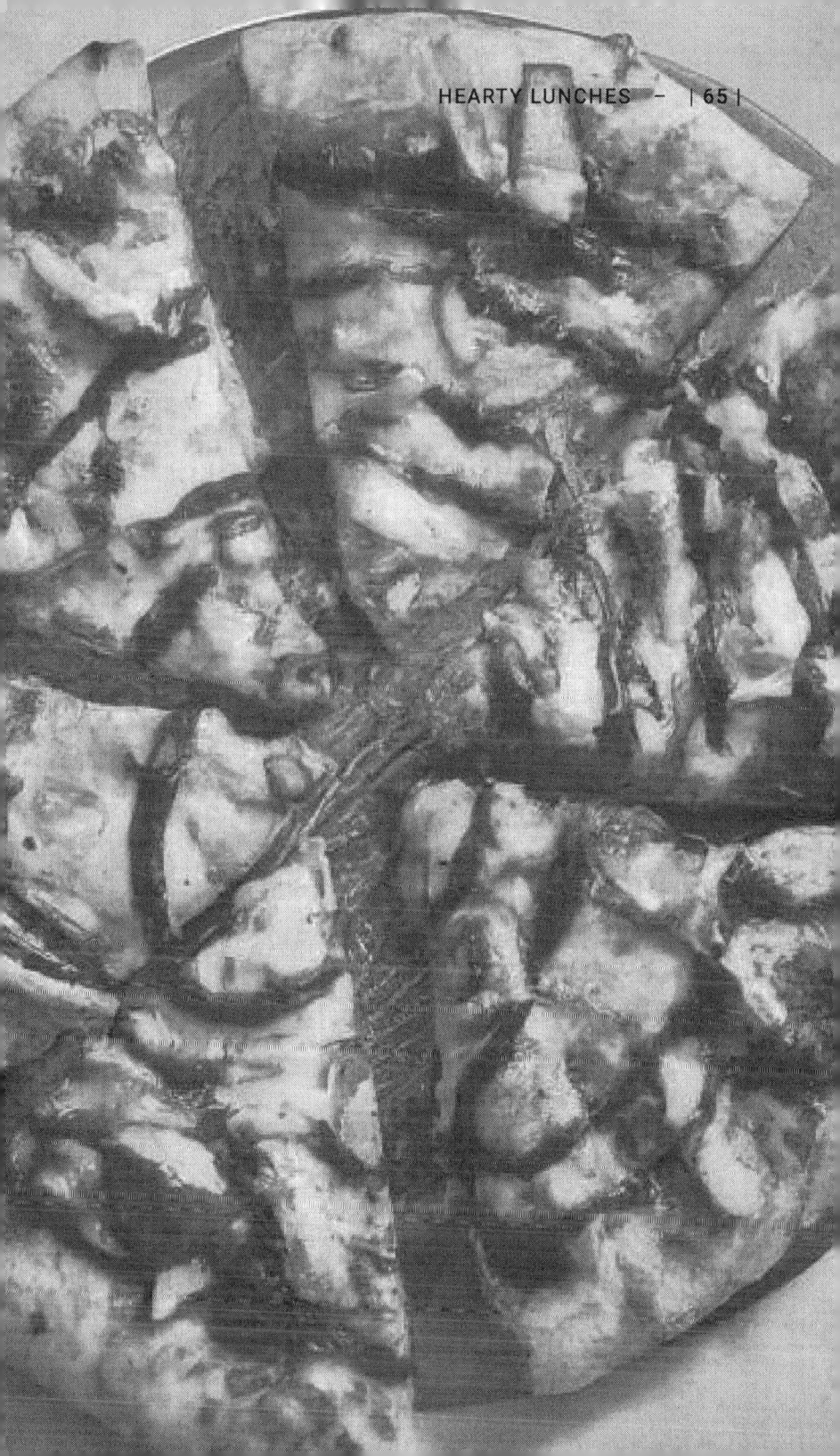

BBQ Chicken Pizza

Servings: 4 | *Prep Time:* 15 mins | *Cook Time:* 15 mins
Ingredients:

- 1 pre-made pizza crust (store-bought or homemade)
- 1/2 cup BBQ sauce
- 2 cups cooked, shredded chicken
- 1 small red onion, thinly sliced
- 1 cup shredded mozzarella cheese
- 1/4 cup chopped fresh cilantro

Instructions:

1. Preheat oven to 450°F (230°C).
2. Spread BBQ sauce evenly over the pizza crust.
3. Top with shredded chicken, red onion, and mozzarella cheese.
4. Bake in preheated oven for 10-15 minutes, or until the crust is golden and the cheese is melted and bubbly.
5. Remove from oven and sprinkle with chopped cilantro before serving.

Nutritional Information:

- Calories: 350
- Protein: 20g
- Carbs: 40g
- Fat: 12g

Cooking Tips:

- For extra flavor, use smoked chicken.
- Add other toppings like bell peppers, jalapeños, or bacon.

Allergen Information:

- Contains gluten and dairy. Use a gluten-free crust and dairy-free cheese if needed.

These hearty lunch recipes are sure to bring a touch of Southern comfort to your mid-day meals. Enjoy the rich flavors and satisfying dishes, and don't forget to share with family and friends!

4

Comforting Dinners

Dinner is a special time when families gather around the table to share not just food, but stories, laughter, and love. It's when the worries of the day melt away and comfort food takes center stage. In the South, dinner is more than a meal; it's a tradition. These recipes are crafted to bring that sense of warmth and togetherness to your table. From hearty meatloaf to flavorful gumbo, these dishes are meant to be savored and shared with those who matter most. So, let's dive into these comforting dinners that will make every evening meal a special occasion.

| 70 | - COMFORTING DINNERS

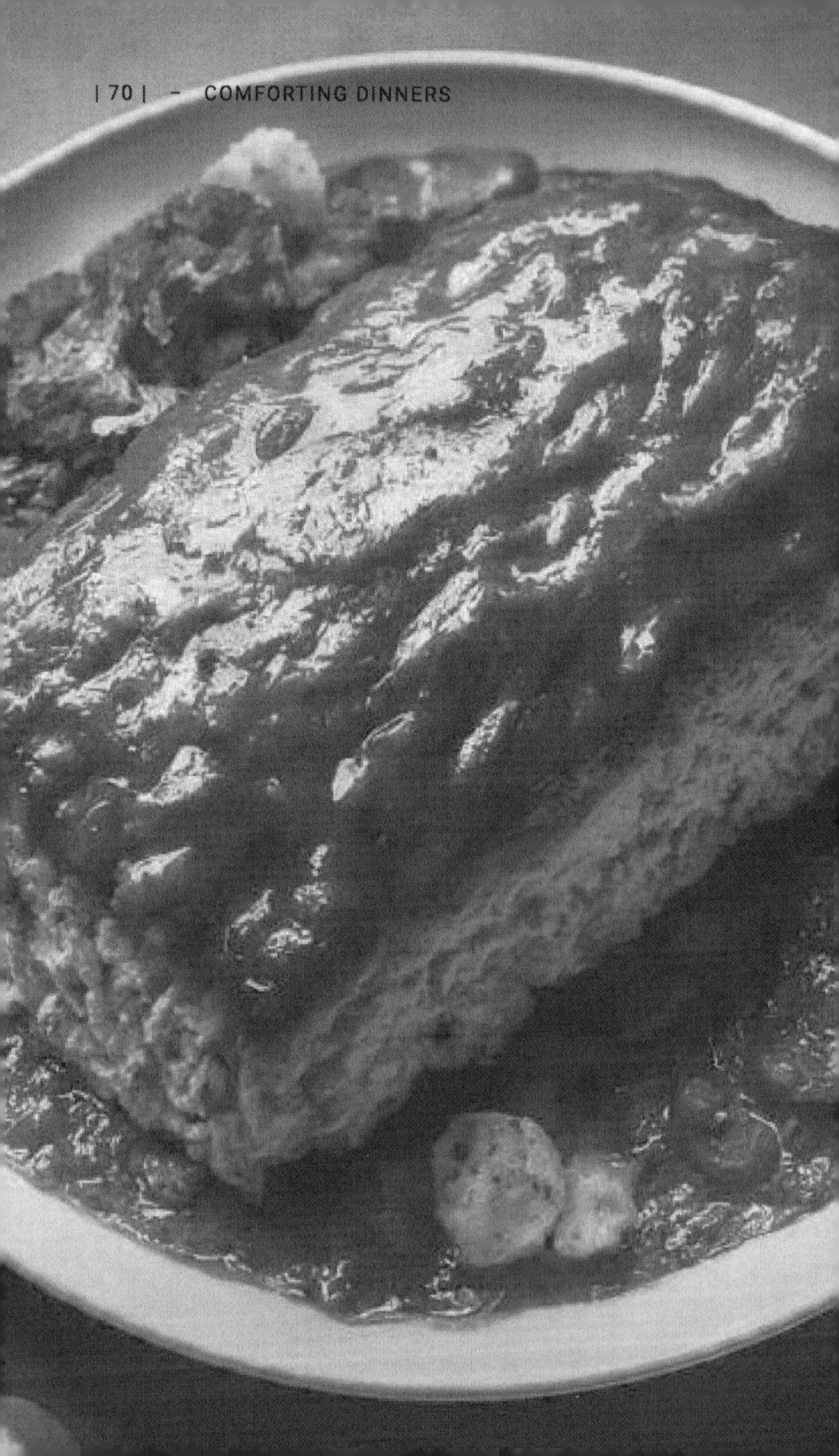

Classic Meatloaf

Servings: 6 | *Prep Time:* 15 mins | *Cook Time:* 1 hr
Ingredients:

- 1 1/2 pounds ground beef
- 1/2 pound ground pork
- 1 onion, finely chopped
- 1/2 cup bread crumbs
- 1/4 cup milk
- 2 large eggs
- 1/4 cup ketchup
- 1 tablespoon Worcestershire sauce
- 1 teaspoon salt
- 1/2 teaspoon black pepper
- 1/2 teaspoon garlic powder
- 1/2 teaspoon dried thyme
- 1/4 cup ketchup (for topping)

Instructions:

1. Preheat oven to 350°F (175°C). Grease a loaf pan.
2. In a large bowl, combine all ingredients except for the 1/4 cup ketchup for topping. Mix until well combined.
3. Transfer the mixture to the prepared loaf pan and shape into a loaf. Spread the remaining ketchup on top.
4. Bake for 1 hour, or until the meatloaf is cooked through and the internal temperature reaches 160°F (70°C).
5. Let rest for 10 minutes before slicing and serving.

Nutritional Information:

- Calories: 400
- Protein: 25g
- Carbs: 15g
- Fat: 25g

Cooking Tips:

- For extra moisture, add a grated carrot or zucchini to the meat mixture.
- Serve with mashed potatoes and green beans for a complete meal.

Allergen Information:

- Contains gluten, dairy, and eggs. Use gluten-free bread crumbs, dairy-free milk, and an egg substitute if needed.

COMFORTING DINNERS — |73|

Chicken and Dumplings

Servings: 6 | *Prep Time:* 20 mins | *Cook Time:* 1 hr
Ingredients:

- 1 whole chicken (about 4 pounds), cut into pieces
- 8 cups chicken broth
- 1 onion, chopped
- 3 carrots, sliced
- 3 celery stalks, sliced
- 1 bay leaf
- Salt and pepper to taste
- 2 cups all-purpose flour
- 1 tablespoon baking powder
- 1/2 teaspoon salt
- 1/2 teaspoon dried thyme
- 1/4 cup cold butter, cubed
- 3/4 cup milk

Instructions:

1. In a large pot, combine chicken, chicken broth, onion, carrots, celery, bay leaf, salt, and pepper. Bring to a boil, then reduce heat and simmer for 45 minutes, or until the chicken is cooked through.
2. Remove chicken from the pot and let cool slightly. Remove and discard the skin and bones, then shred the meat.
3. Return the shredded chicken to the pot. Discard the bay leaf.

4. In a large bowl, combine flour, baking powder, salt, and thyme. Cut in the butter until the mixture resembles coarse crumbs. Stir in the milk until just combined.
5. Drop spoonfuls of the dough into the simmering broth. Cover and simmer for 15 minutes, or until the dumplings are cooked through.
6. Serve hot.

Nutritional Information:

- Calories: 500
- Protein: 35g
- Carbs: 35g
- Fat: 20g

Cooking Tips:

- For extra flavor, add a splash of heavy cream to the broth.
- Garnish with fresh parsley or chives before serving.

Allergen Information:

- Contains gluten and dairy. Use gluten-free flour and dairy-free milk if needed.

– COMFORTING DINNERS

Beef Stew with Vegetables

Servings: 6 | *Prep Time:* 20 mins | *Cook Time:* 2 hrs
Ingredients:

- 2 pounds beef stew meat, cut into 1-inch cubes
- 2 tablespoons vegetable oil
- 1 onion, chopped
- 3 cloves garlic, minced
- 6 cups beef broth
- 3 carrots, sliced
- 3 potatoes, diced
- 2 celery stalks, sliced
- 1 cup frozen peas
- 1 bay leaf
- 1 teaspoon dried thyme
- Salt and pepper to taste
- 2 tablespoons cornstarch
- 2 tablespoons water

Instructions:

1. In a large pot, heat vegetable oil over medium-high heat. Add beef and cook until browned on all sides. Remove from the pot and set aside.
2. In the same pot, add onion and garlic and cook until softened, about 5 minutes.
3. Return beef to the pot and add beef broth, carrots, potatoes, celery, bay leaf, thyme, salt, and pepper. Bring to a boil, then

reduce heat and simmer for 1 1/2 to 2 hours, or until the beef is tender.
4. Stir in frozen peas and cook for another 5 minutes.
5. In a small bowl, mix cornstarch and water until smooth. Stir into the stew and cook until the stew has thickened.
6. Serve hot.

Nutritional Information:

- Calories: 450
- Protein: 30g
- Carbs: 35g
- Fat: 20g

Cooking Tips:

- For a richer flavor, use red wine instead of some of the beef broth.
- Add other vegetables like mushrooms or parsnips for extra nutrition.

Allergen Information:

- Gluten-free.

COMFORTING DINNERS — | 79 |

Southern Fried Catfish

Servings: 4 | *Prep Time:* 10 mins | *Cook Time:* 15 mins
Ingredients:

- 4 catfish fillets
- 1 cup buttermilk
- 1 cup cornmeal
- 1/2 cup all-purpose flour
- 1 teaspoon paprika
- 1 teaspoon garlic powder
- 1 teaspoon salt
- 1/2 teaspoon black pepper
- 1/2 teaspoon cayenne pepper
- Vegetable oil, for frying
- Lemon wedges, for serving

Instructions:

1. Place catfish fillets in a large bowl and cover with buttermilk. Let soak for 10 minutes.
2. In a shallow dish, combine cornmeal, flour, paprika, garlic powder, salt, black pepper, and cayenne pepper.
3. Heat vegetable oil in a large skillet over medium-high heat.
4. Remove catfish fillets from buttermilk, letting excess drip off, and dredge in the cornmeal mixture, coating completely.
5. Fry the catfish fillets in the hot oil until golden brown and cooked through, about 5-7 minutes per side. Remove and drain on paper towels.
6. Serve hot with lemon wedges.

Nutritional Information:

- Calories: 450
- Protein: 25g
- Carbs: 40g
- Fat: 20g

Cooking Tips:

- For extra crispiness, double-dip the fillets in buttermilk and cornmeal.
- Serve with tartar sauce or hot sauce for added flavor.

Allergen Information:

- Contains gluten and dairy. Use gluten-free flour and a dairy-free buttermilk alternative if needed.

— COMFORTING DINNERS

Baked Macaroni and Cheese

Servings: 8 | *Prep Time:* 15 mins | *Cook Time:* 30 mins
Ingredients:

- 8 ounces elbow macaroni
- 4 tablespoons butter
- 1/4 cup all-purpose flour
- 2 cups milk
- 2 cups shredded cheddar cheese
- 1 cup shredded mozzarella cheese
- 1/2 teaspoon salt
- 1/4 teaspoon black pepper
- 1/4 cup grated Parmesan cheese
- 1/2 cup bread crumbs

Instructions:

1. Preheat oven to 350°F (175°C). Grease a 9x13-inch baking dish.
2. Cook macaroni according to package instructions. Drain and set aside.
3. In a large saucepan, melt butter over medium heat. Stir in flour and cook until bubbly, about 1 minute.
4. Gradually whisk in milk and cook, stirring constantly, until the mixture is thickened and bubbly.
5. Remove from heat and stir in cheddar cheese, mozzarella cheese, salt, and pepper until melted and smooth.
6. Add cooked macaroni to the cheese sauce and stir until well coated.

7. Pour the macaroni and cheese into the prepared baking dish. In a small bowl, combine Parmesan cheese and bread crumbs. Sprinkle over the top.
8. Bake for 25-30 minutes, or until the top is golden brown and the sauce is bubbly.

Nutritional Information:

- Calories: 400
- Protein: 15g
- Carbs: 45g
- Fat: 18g

Cooking Tips:

- For a smoky flavor, use smoked cheddar cheese.
- Add cooked bacon or ham for extra protein and flavor.

Allergen Information:

- Contains gluten and dairy. Use gluten-free pasta and flour, and dairy-free cheese and milk if needed.

BBQ Ribs

Servings: 6 | *Prep Time:* 15 mins | *Cook Time:* 3 hrs
Ingredients:

- 3 pounds pork ribs
- 1/4 cup brown sugar
- 1 tablespoon paprika
- 1 tablespoon garlic powder

- 1 tablespoon onion powder
- 1 teaspoon salt
- 1 teaspoon black pepper
- 1 teaspoon cayenne pepper
- 2 cups BBQ sauce

Instructions:

1. Preheat oven to 300°F (150°C).
2. In a small bowl, combine brown sugar, paprika, garlic powder, onion powder, salt, black pepper, and cayenne pepper.
3. Rub the spice mixture all over the ribs.
4. Place the ribs on a baking sheet lined with foil. Cover tightly with foil and bake for 2 1/2 hours.
5. Remove the foil and brush the ribs with BBQ sauce. Increase oven temperature to 375°F (190°C) and bake for an additional 30 minutes, or until the ribs are tender and the sauce is caramelized.
6. Let rest for 10 minutes before slicing and serving.

Nutritional Information:

- Calories: 500
- Protein: 30g
- Carbs: 30g
- Fat: 25g

Cooking Tips:

- For extra smoky flavor, cook the ribs on a grill instead of the oven.

- Serve with coleslaw and cornbread for a complete meal.

Allergen Information:

- Gluten-free.

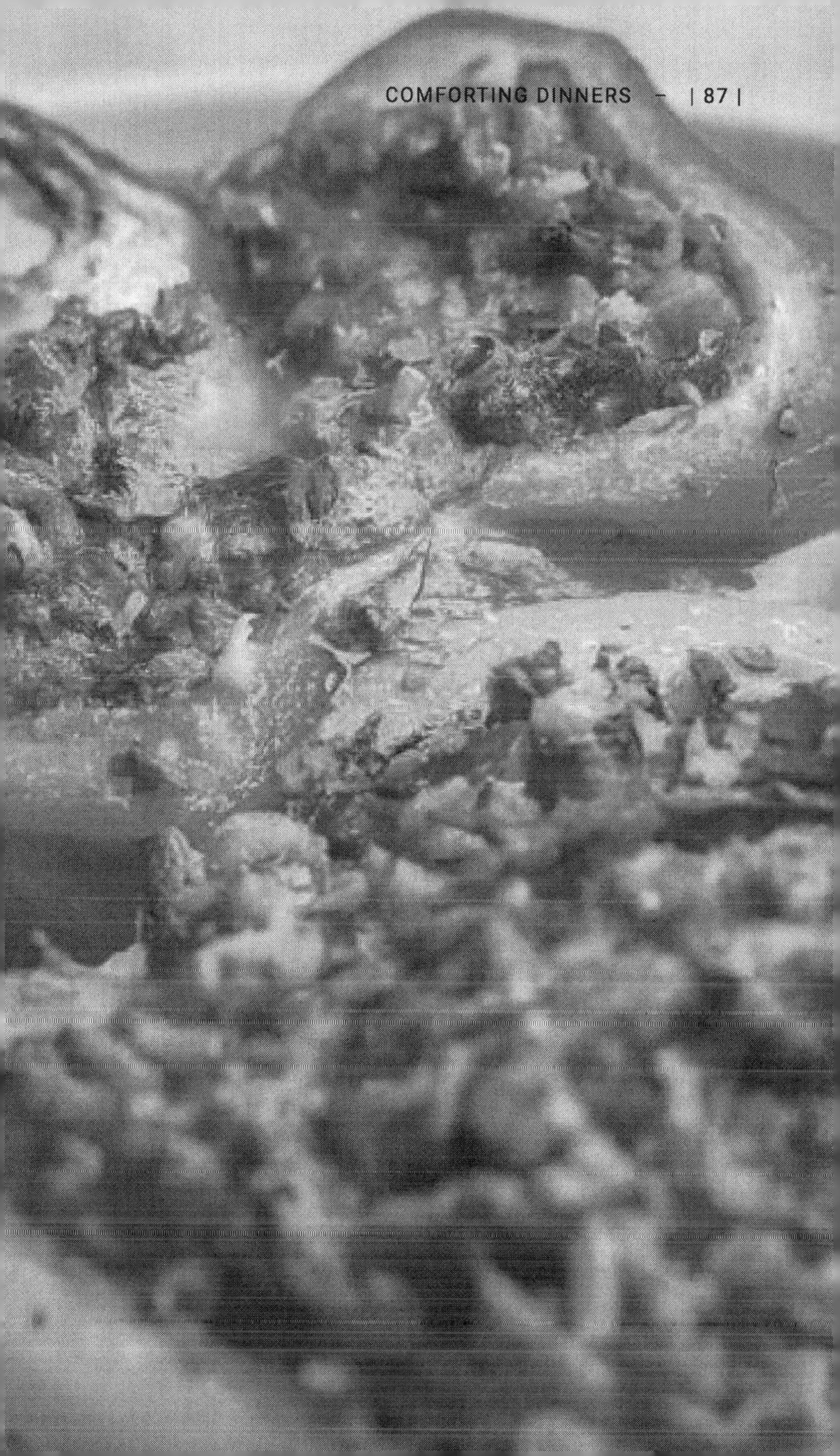

Stuffed Bell Peppers

Servings: 4 | *Prep Time:* 15 mins | *Cook Time:* 45 mins
Ingredients:

- 4 large bell peppers
- 1 pound ground beef
- 1 small onion, chopped
- 2 cloves garlic, minced
- 1 cup cooked rice
- 1 cup tomato sauce
- 1 cup shredded cheddar cheese
- 1 teaspoon salt
- 1/2 teaspoon black pepper
- 1/2 teaspoon dried oregano

Instructions:

1. Preheat oven to 375°F (190°C).
2. Cut the tops off the bell peppers and remove the seeds and membranes. Set aside.
3. In a large skillet, cook ground beef, onion, and garlic over medium heat until the beef is browned and the onion is softened. Drain any excess fat.
4. Stir in cooked rice, tomato sauce, 1/2 cup shredded cheese, salt, black pepper, and oregano.
5. Spoon the beef mixture into the bell peppers and place them in a baking dish.
6. Sprinkle the remaining 1/2 cup shredded cheese over the top of the stuffed peppers.

7. Cover with foil and bake for 30 minutes. Remove the foil and bake for an additional 15 minutes, or until the peppers are tender and the cheese is melted and bubbly.
8. Serve hot.

Nutritional Information:

- Calories: 350
- Protein: 20g
- Carbs: 25g
- Fat: 20g

Cooking Tips:

- For a lighter version, use ground turkey or chicken instead of beef.
- Add other vegetables like mushrooms or zucchini to the filling for extra nutrition.

Allergen Information:

- Contains dairy. Use dairy-free cheese if needed.

| 90 | - COMFORTING DINNERS

Jambalaya

Servings: 6 | *Prep Time:* 15 mins | *Cook Time:* 45 mins
Ingredients:

- 2 tablespoons vegetable oil
- 1 pound chicken breast, diced
- 1 pound Andouille sausage, sliced
- 1 onion, chopped
- 1 bell pepper, chopped
- 2 celery stalks, chopped
- 3 cloves garlic, minced
- 2 cups long-grain rice
- 4 cups chicken broth
- 1 (14.5-ounce) can diced tomatoes
- 2 teaspoons paprika
- 1 teaspoon dried thyme
- 1 teaspoon dried oregano
- 1/2 teaspoon cayenne pepper
- 1/2 teaspoon salt
- 1/2 teaspoon black pepper
- 1 pound shrimp, peeled and deveined

Instructions:

1. In a large pot, heat vegetable oil over medium-high heat. Add chicken and sausage, and cook until browned. Remove from the pot and set aside.
2. In the same pot, add onion, bell pepper, celery, and garlic. Cook until softened, about 5 minutes.

3. Stir in rice and cook for 2 minutes, until lightly toasted.
4. Add chicken broth, diced tomatoes, paprika, thyme, oregano, cayenne pepper, salt, and black pepper. Bring to a boil, then reduce heat and simmer for 20 minutes, or until the rice is tender and the liquid is absorbed.
5. Stir in the cooked chicken, sausage, and shrimp. Cook for another 5-7 minutes, or until the shrimp are pink and cooked through.
6. Serve hot.

Nutritional Information:

- Calories: 450
- Protein: 30g
- Carbs: 45g
- Fat: 15g

Cooking Tips:

- For extra flavor, use smoked sausage.
- Add hot sauce for a spicier jambalaya.

Allergen Information:

- Contains shellfish. Omit shrimp if needed.

COMFORTING DINNERS — |93|

Gumbo

Servings: 6 | *Prep Time:* 20 mins | *Cook Time:* 1 hr 30 mins
Ingredients:

- 1/2 cup vegetable oil
- 1/2 cup all-purpose flour
- 1 onion, chopped
- 1 bell pepper, chopped
- 2 celery stalks, chopped
- 4 cloves garlic, minced
- 1 pound Andouille sausage, sliced
- 1 pound chicken thighs, diced
- 6 cups chicken broth
- 1 (14.5-ounce) can diced tomatoes
- 1 teaspoon dried thyme
- 1 teaspoon dried oregano
- 1/2 teaspoon cayenne pepper
- 1/2 teaspoon salt
- 1/2 teaspoon black pepper
- 1 pound shrimp, peeled and deveined
- 2 cups cooked rice
- 1/4 cup chopped fresh parsley

Instructions:

1. In a large pot, heat vegetable oil over medium-high heat. Whisk in flour and cook, stirring constantly, until the mixture turns a deep brown color, about 10-15 minutes.

2. Add onion, bell pepper, celery, and garlic. Cook until softened, about 5 minutes.
3. Stir in sausage and chicken, and cook until browned.
4. Add chicken broth, diced tomatoes, thyme, oregano, cayenne pepper, salt, and black pepper. Bring to a boil, then reduce heat and simmer for 45 minutes.
5. Stir in shrimp and cook for another 5-7 minutes, or until the shrimp are pink and cooked through.
6. Serve gumbo over cooked rice, garnished with fresh parsley.

Nutritional Information:

- Calories: 500
- Protein: 30g
- Carbs: 40g
- Fat: 20g

Cooking Tips:

- For a richer flavor, use seafood stock instead of chicken broth.
- Add okra for a traditional touch.

Allergen Information:

- Contains gluten and shellfish. Use gluten-free flour and omit shrimp if needed.

| 96 | – COMFORTING DINNERS

Chicken Fried Steak

Servings: 4 | *Prep Time:* 15 mins | *Cook Time:* 20 mins
Ingredients:

- 4 beef cube steaks
- 1 cup all-purpose flour
- 1 teaspoon salt
- 1/2 teaspoon black pepper
- 1/2 teaspoon paprika
- 1/2 teaspoon garlic powder
- 2 large eggs
- 1 cup buttermilk
- 1 cup vegetable oil, for frying
- 2 cups milk
- 2 tablespoons all-purpose flour
- Salt and pepper to taste

Instructions:

1. In a shallow dish, combine 1 cup flour, salt, black pepper, paprika, and garlic powder.
2. In another shallow dish, whisk together eggs and buttermilk.
3. Dredge each steak in the flour mixture, then dip in the egg mixture, and dredge again in the flour mixture.
4. Heat vegetable oil in a large skillet over medium-high heat. Fry the steaks until golden brown and cooked through, about 4-5 minutes per side. Remove and drain on paper towels.
5. Pour off all but 2 tablespoons of the oil from the skillet. Whisk in 2 tablespoons flour and cook until bubbly. Gradually whisk

in milk and cook, stirring constantly, until the gravy is thickened. Season with salt and pepper.
6. Serve the chicken fried steak with the gravy.

Nutritional Information:

- Calories: 600
- Protein: 30g
- Carbs: 40g
- Fat: 35g

Cooking Tips:

- For extra crispy steaks, double-dip in the flour mixture.
- Serve with mashed potatoes and green beans for a complete meal.

Allergen Information:

- Contains gluten and dairy. Use gluten-free flour and a dairy-free buttermilk alternative if needed.

5

Savory Sides

In Southern cuisine, side dishes are more than just an accompaniment to the main course—they are a vital part of the meal that brings balance and flavor to the table. These savory sides, often rich in tradition and taste, can turn a simple meal into a feast. From crispy cornbread to creamy potato salad, each dish tells a story and carries the essence of Southern hospitality. These recipes will help you create sides that not only complement your meals but also stand out on their own. So, let's dive into these classic Southern sides that are sure to become staples in your kitchen.

| 100 | — SAVORY SIDES

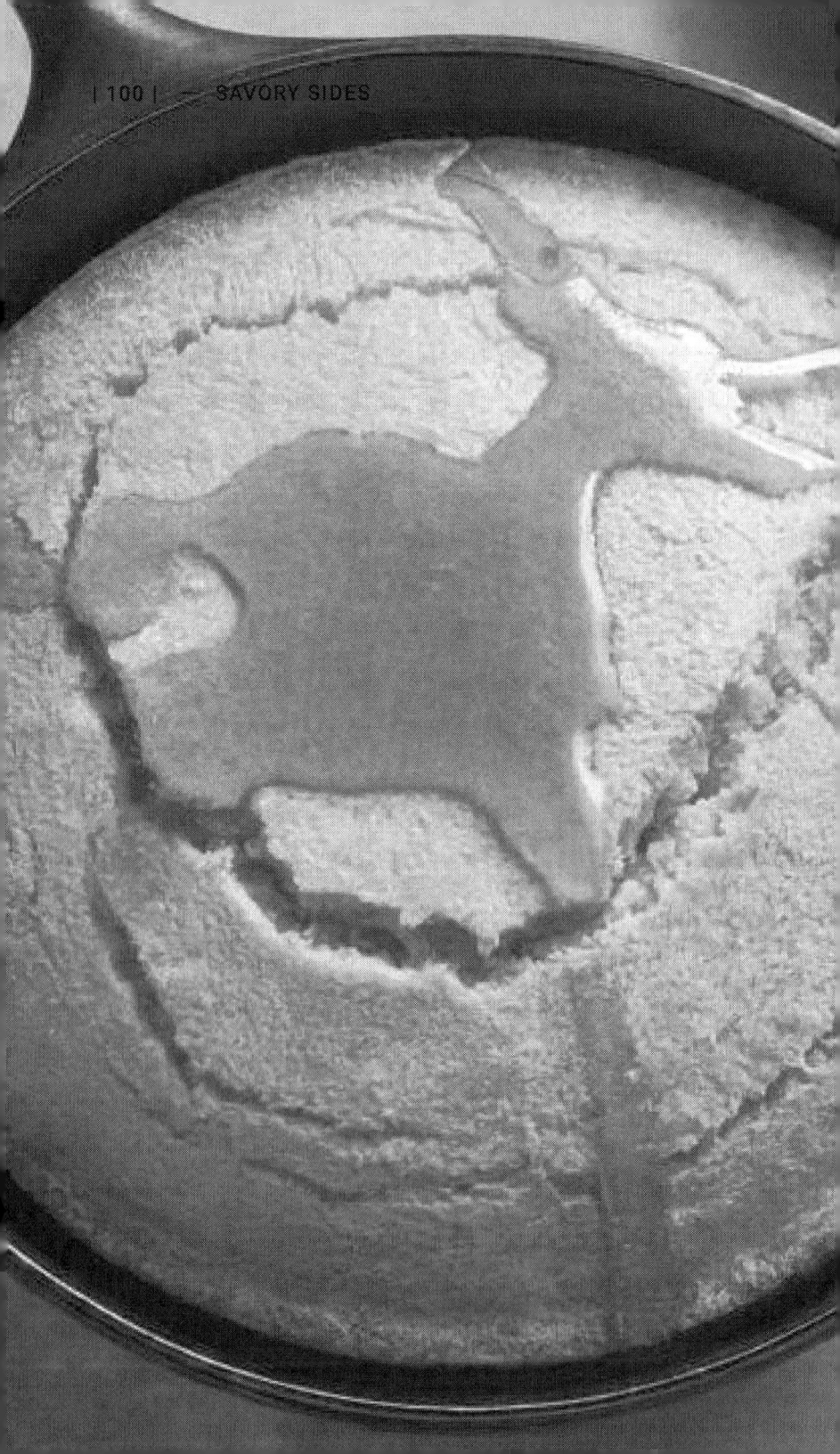

Cornbread

Servings: 8 | *Prep Time:* 10 mins | *Cook Time:* 20 mins
Ingredients:

- 1 cup cornmeal
- 1 cup all-purpose flour
- 1/4 cup sugar
- 1 tablespoon baking powder
- 1/2 teaspoon salt
- 1 cup buttermilk
- 1/2 cup melted butter
- 2 large eggs

Instructions:

1. Preheat oven to 400°F (200°C). Grease an 8-inch square baking dish or a cast-iron skillet.
2. In a large bowl, whisk together cornmeal, flour, sugar, baking powder, and salt.
3. In another bowl, whisk together buttermilk, melted butter, and eggs. Pour the wet ingredients into the dry ingredients and stir until just combined.
4. Pour the batter into the prepared baking dish or skillet.
5. Bake for 20-25 minutes, or until golden brown and a toothpick inserted into the center comes out clean.
6. Let cool slightly before serving.

Nutritional Information:

- Calories: 250
- Protein: 5g
- Carbs: 35g
- Fat: 10g

Cooking Tips:

- For a sweeter cornbread, increase the sugar to 1/2 cup.
- Add corn kernels or jalapeños for extra flavor and texture.

Allergen Information:

- Contains gluten, dairy, and eggs. Use gluten-free flour, dairy-free buttermilk, and an egg substitute if needed.

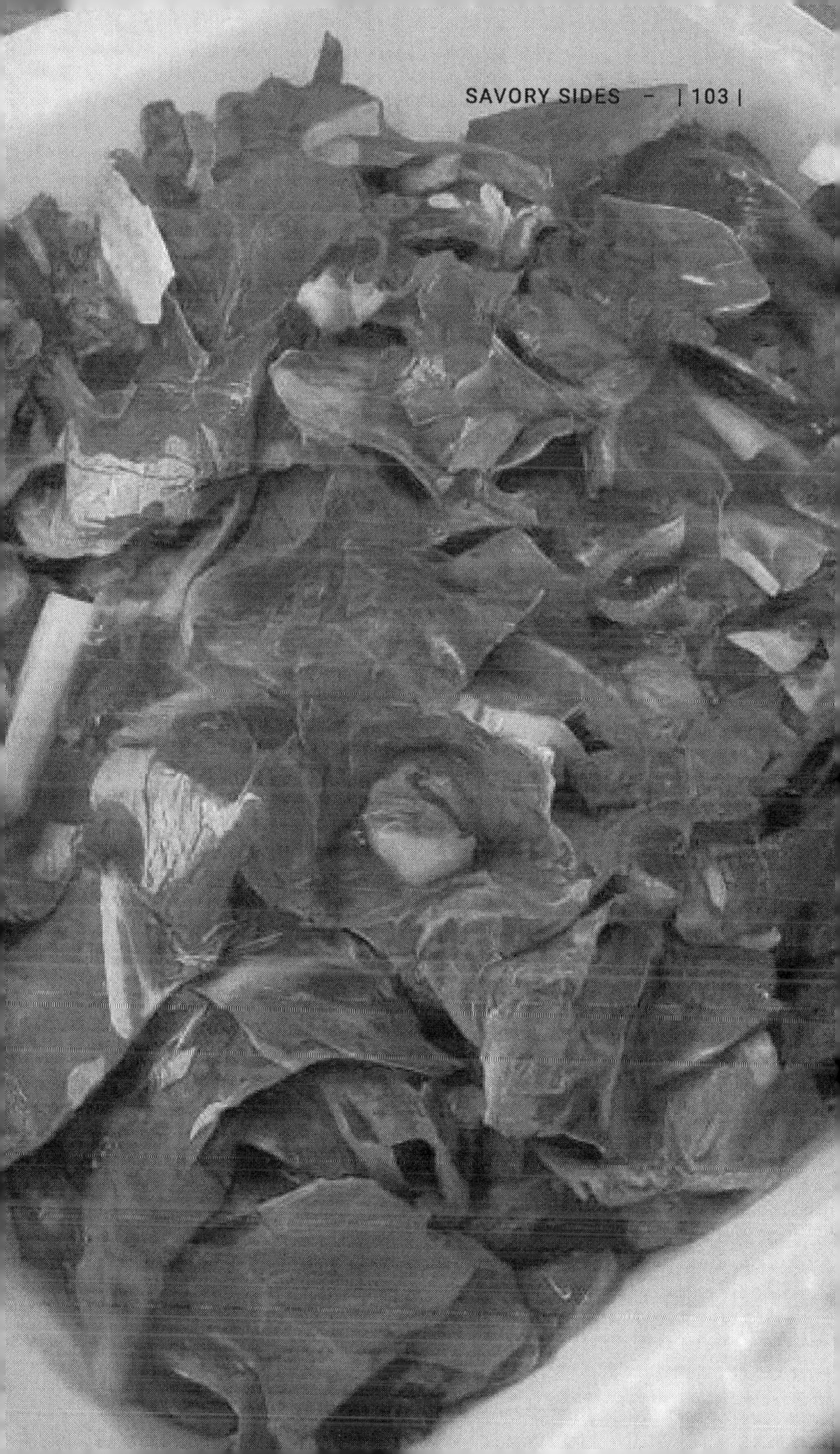

Collard Greens

Servings: 6 | *Prep Time:* 15 mins | *Cook Time:* 1 hr
Ingredients:

- 1 tablespoon olive oil
- 1 onion, chopped
- 2 cloves garlic, minced
- 1 ham hock or 4 slices bacon
- 2 pounds collard greens, trimmed and chopped
- 4 cups chicken broth
- 1 tablespoon apple cider vinegar
- 1 teaspoon sugar
- Salt and pepper to taste

Instructions:

1. In a large pot, heat olive oil over medium heat. Add onion and garlic, and cook until softened, about 5 minutes.
2. Add ham hock or bacon and cook for another 5 minutes.
3. Stir in collard greens, chicken broth, apple cider vinegar, and sugar. Bring to a boil, then reduce heat and simmer for 45 minutes to 1 hour, or until the greens are tender.
4. Season with salt and pepper to taste and serve hot.

Nutritional Information:

- Calories: 150
- Protein: 8g
- Carbs: 10g

- Fat: 8g

Cooking Tips:

- For a vegetarian version, omit the ham hock or bacon and use vegetable broth.
- Add a pinch of red pepper flakes for a spicy kick.

Allergen Information:

- Gluten-free. Use gluten-free broth if needed.

SAVORY SIDES

Baked Beans

Servings: 8 | *Prep Time:* 15 mins | *Cook Time:* 2 hrs
Ingredients:

- 4 slices bacon, chopped
- 1 onion, chopped
- 2 cloves garlic, minced
- 4 (15-ounce) cans navy beans, drained and rinsed
- 1/2 cup ketchup
- 1/4 cup molasses
- 1/4 cup brown sugar
- 2 tablespoons mustard
- 1 tablespoon Worcestershire sauce
- 1/2 teaspoon salt
- 1/2 teaspoon black pepper

Instructions:

1. Preheat oven to 350°F (175°C).
2. In a large skillet, cook bacon over medium heat until crispy. Remove bacon and set aside, leaving the drippings in the skillet.
3. Add onion and garlic to the skillet and cook until softened, about 5 minutes.
4. In a large bowl, combine beans, cooked onion and garlic, bacon, ketchup, molasses, brown sugar, mustard, Worcestershire sauce, salt, and pepper. Mix well.
5. Transfer the mixture to a greased 9x13-inch baking dish.

6. Bake for 1 1/2 to 2 hours, or until the beans are thick and bubbly. Let cool slightly before serving.

Nutritional Information:

- Calories: 250
- Protein: 8g
- Carbs: 40g
- Fat: 5g

Cooking Tips:

- For a smokier flavor, use smoked bacon or add a dash of liquid smoke.
- Adjust the sweetness by adding more or less brown sugar to taste.

Allergen Information:

- Gluten-free. Use gluten-free Worcestershire sauce if needed.

SAVORY SIDES — | 109 |

Creamed Corn

Servings: 6 | *Prep Time:* 10 mins | *Cook Time:* 15 mins
Ingredients:

- 4 cups fresh or frozen corn kernels
- 1 cup heavy cream
- 1/2 cup milk
- 2 tablespoons butter
- 1 tablespoon sugar
- 1 teaspoon salt
- 1/2 teaspoon black pepper
- 2 tablespoons all-purpose flour

Instructions:

1. In a large skillet, combine corn, heavy cream, milk, butter, sugar, salt, and pepper. Cook over medium heat until the mixture is hot and bubbling, about 5 minutes.
2. In a small bowl, whisk together the flour and a few tablespoons of the hot liquid from the skillet until smooth. Stir the flour mixture back into the skillet.
3. Continue to cook, stirring frequently, until the creamed corn is thickened, about 10 minutes.
4. Serve hot.

Nutritional Information:

- Calories: 200
- Protein: 4g

- Carbs: 24g
- Fat: 10g

Cooking Tips:

- For a richer flavor, use half-and-half instead of milk.
- Add a pinch of cayenne pepper for a spicy kick.

Allergen Information:

- Contains dairy and gluten. Use dairy-free milk and cream, and gluten-free flour if needed.

— SAVORY SIDES

Potato Salad

Servings: 8 | *Prep Time:* 20 mins | *Cook Time:* 15 mins

Ingredients:

- 4 large potatoes, peeled and diced
- 4 large eggs, hard-boiled and chopped
- 1 cup mayonnaise
- 1/4 cup Dijon mustard
- 1/4 cup chopped dill pickles
- 1/4 cup chopped red onion
- 1/4 cup chopped celery
- Salt and pepper to taste

Instructions:

1. In a large pot, boil potatoes until tender, about 10-15 minutes. Drain and let cool slightly.
2. In a large bowl, combine potatoes, chopped eggs, mayonnaise, Dijon mustard, dill pickles, red onion, and celery. Mix well.
3. Season with salt and pepper to taste.
4. Chill in the refrigerator for at least 1 hour before serving.

Nutritional Information:

- Calories: 250
- Protein: 5g
- Carbs: 30g
- Fat: 13g

Cooking Tips:

- For a tangier salad, add a splash of pickle juice.
- Use Yukon Gold or red potatoes for a creamier texture.

Allergen Information:

- Contains eggs. Use an egg-free mayonnaise if needed.

Sweet Potato Casserole

Servings: 8 | *Prep Time:* 15 mins | *Cook Time:* 30 mins

Ingredients:

- 4 large sweet potatoes, peeled and diced
- 1/2 cup brown sugar
- 1/4 cup melted butter
- 1 teaspoon vanilla extract
- 1/2 teaspoon ground cinnamon
- 1/4 teaspoon ground nutmeg
- 1/4 teaspoon salt
- 1/2 cup chopped pecans
- 1/2 cup mini marshmallows

Instructions:

1. Preheat oven to 350°F (175°C).
2. In a large pot, boil sweet potatoes until tender, about 15 minutes. Drain and mash until smooth.
3. In a large bowl, combine mashed sweet potatoes, brown sugar, melted butter, vanilla extract, cinnamon, nutmeg, and salt. Mix well.
4. Transfer the sweet potato mixture to a greased 9x13-inch baking dish. Top with chopped pecans and mini marshmallows.
5. Bake for 20-25 minutes, or until the top is golden brown and the marshmallows are melted.
6. Let cool slightly before serving.

Nutritional Information:

- Calories: 300
- Protein: 3g
- Carbs: 50g
- Fat: 12g

Cooking Tips:

- For a less sweet version, reduce the amount of brown sugar.
- Add a pinch of ground cloves or ginger for extra warmth and spice.

Allergen Information:

- Contains nuts and dairy. Omit nuts and use dairy-free butter if needed.

Deviled Eggs

Servings: 12 halves | *Prep Time:* 15 mins | *Cook Time:* 10 mins

Ingredients:

- 6 large eggs
- 1/4 cup mayonnaise
- 1 teaspoon Dijon mustard
- 1 teaspoon white vinegar
- 1/2 teaspoon salt
- 1/4 teaspoon black pepper
- Paprika, for garnish

Instructions:

1. Place eggs in a saucepan and cover with water. Bring to a boil, then remove from heat, cover, and let sit for 10 minutes. Drain and cool the eggs under cold running water.
2. Peel the eggs and cut in half lengthwise. Remove the yolks and place them in a bowl.
3. Mash the yolks with mayonnaise, Dijon mustard, vinegar, salt, and pepper until smooth.
4. Spoon or pipe the yolk mixture back into the egg whites.
5. Sprinkle with paprika before serving.

Nutritional Information:

- Calories: 80
- Protein: 4g
- Carbs: 1g
- Fat: 7g

Cooking Tips:

- For extra flavor, add finely chopped pickles or a dash of hot sauce to the yolk mixture.
- Use a piping bag for a more decorative presentation.

Allergen Information:

- Contains eggs. Use an egg-free mayonnaise if needed.

| 118 | – SAVORY SIDES

Hush Puppies

Servings: 12 | *Prep Time:* 10 mins | *Cook Time:* 15 mins
Ingredients:

- 1 cup cornmeal
- 1/2 cup all-purpose flour
- 1/4 cup sugar
- 1 teaspoon baking powder
- 1/2 teaspoon salt
- 1/4 teaspoon baking soda
- 1/4 teaspoon garlic powder
- 1/4 teaspoon onion powder
- 1/2 cup buttermilk
- 1 large egg
- 1/4 cup grated onion
- Vegetable oil, for frying

Instructions:

1. In a large bowl, whisk together cornmeal, flour, sugar, baking powder, salt, baking soda, garlic powder, and onion powder.
2. In another bowl, whisk together buttermilk and egg. Pour the wet ingredients into the dry ingredients and stir until just combined. Fold in the grated onion.
3. Heat vegetable oil in a deep fryer or large pot to 350°F (175°C).
4. Drop spoonfuls of the batter into the hot oil and fry until golden brown, about 2-3 minutes per side. Remove and drain on paper towels.

5. Serve hot.

Nutritional Information:

- Calories: 150
- Protein: 3g
- Carbs: 20g
- Fat: 6g

Cooking Tips:

- For a spicier version, add a pinch of cayenne pepper to the batter.
- Serve with honey or dipping sauce for extra flavor.

Allergen Information:

- Contains gluten, dairy, and eggs. Use gluten-free flour, dairy-free buttermilk, and an egg substitute if needed.

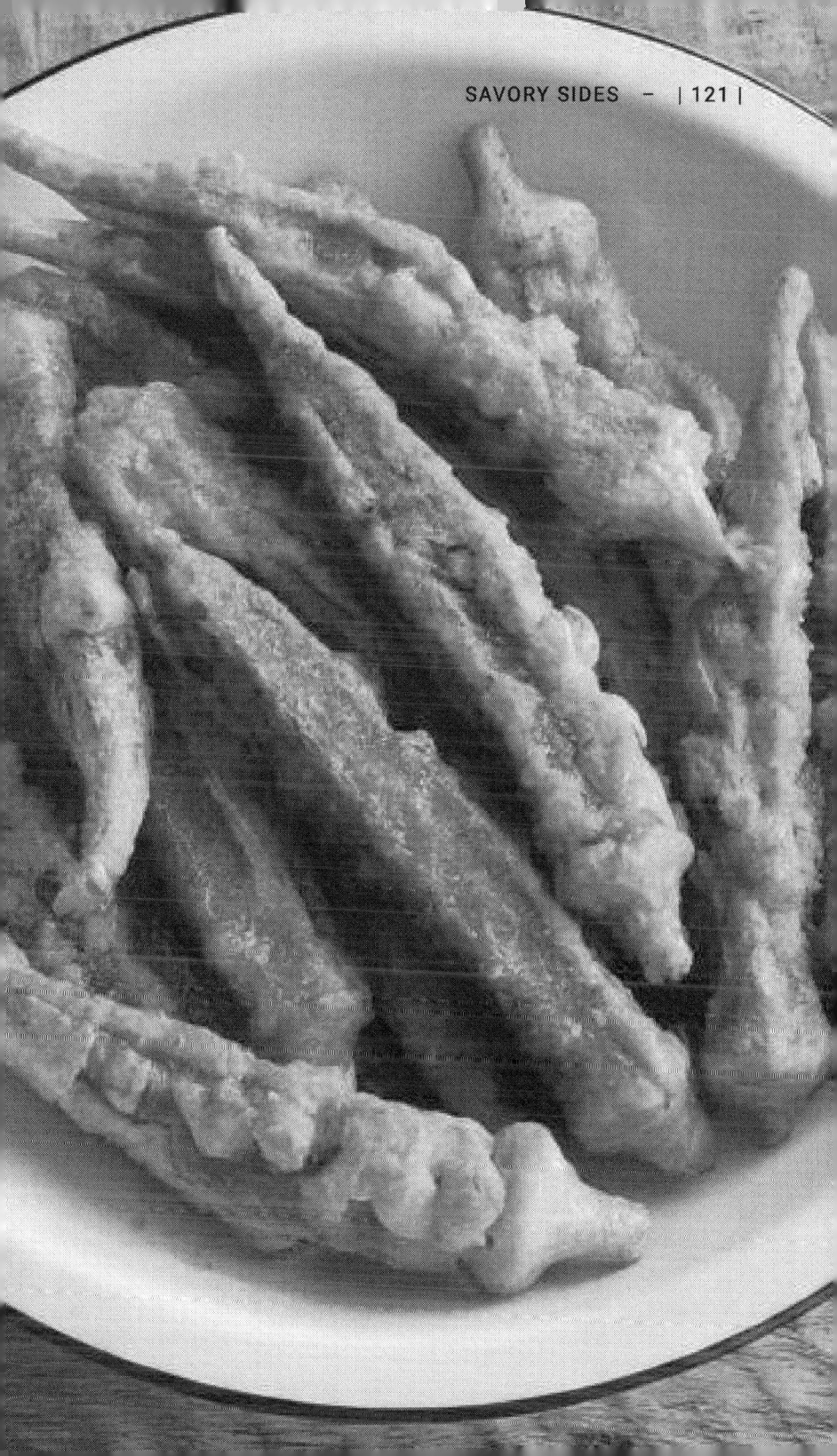

SAVORY SIDES — | 121 |

Fried Okra

Servings: 6 | *Prep Time:* 10 mins | *Cook Time:* 15 mins
Ingredients:

- 1 pound fresh okra, cut into 1/2-inch pieces
- 1 cup buttermilk
- 1 cup cornmeal
- 1/2 cup all-purpose flour
- 1 teaspoon salt
- 1/2 teaspoon black pepper
- 1/2 teaspoon paprika
- Vegetable oil, for frying

Instructions:

1. In a large bowl, soak the okra pieces in buttermilk for 10 minutes.
2. In another bowl, combine cornmeal, flour, salt, black pepper, and paprika.
3. Heat vegetable oil in a deep fryer or large pot to 350°F (175°C).
4. Remove the okra from the buttermilk, letting excess drip off, and dredge in the cornmeal mixture, coating completely.
5. Fry the okra in the hot oil until golden brown, about 2-3 minutes. Remove and drain on paper towels.
6. Serve hot.

Nutritional Information:

- Calories: 200
- Protein: 4g
- Carbs: 30g
- Fat: 8g

Cooking Tips:

- For extra crunch, double-dip the okra in buttermilk and cornmeal.
- Serve with a side of ranch dressing for dipping.

Allergen Information:

- Contains gluten and dairy. Use gluten-free flour and a dairy-free buttermilk alternative if needed.

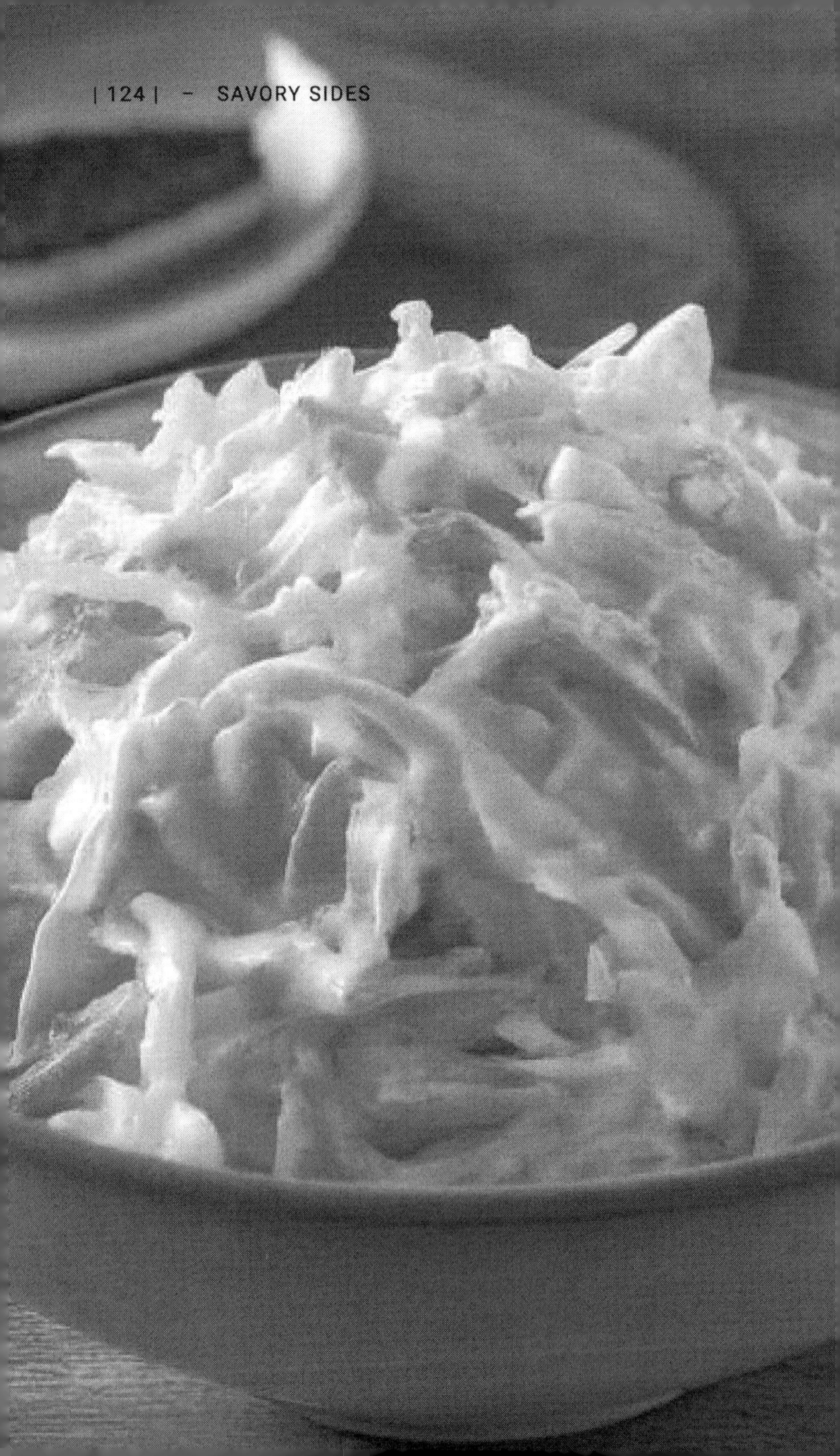

Southern Coleslaw

Servings: 8 | *Prep Time:* 15 mins | *Cook Time:* 0 mins
Ingredients:

- 1 small head green cabbage, shredded
- 1 carrot, grated
- 1/4 cup chopped red onion
- 1/2 cup mayonnaise
- 1/4 cup apple cider vinegar
- 2 tablespoons sugar
- 1 teaspoon Dijon mustard
- 1/2 teaspoon celery seed
- Salt and pepper to taste

Instructions:

1. In a large bowl, combine shredded cabbage, grated carrot, and chopped red onion.
2. In another bowl, whisk together mayonnaise, apple cider vinegar, sugar, Dijon mustard, celery seed, salt, and pepper.
3. Pour the dressing over the cabbage mixture and toss to coat.
4. Chill in the refrigerator for at least 1 hour before serving.

Nutritional Information:

- Calories: 150
- Protein: 2g
- Carbs: 10g
- Fat: 12g

Cooking Tips:

- For a lighter coleslaw, use Greek yogurt instead of mayonnaise.
- Add a splash of lemon juice for extra tanginess.

Allergen Information:

- Contains eggs. Use an egg-free mayonnaise if needed.

6

Sweet Treats

Desserts in the South are more than just the end of a meal; they're a celebration of sweetness, tradition, and love. From church picnics to Sunday dinners, sweet treats have always held a special place in our hearts and kitchens. These desserts are not just about satisfying a sweet tooth; they're about creating memories, sharing joy, and indulging in the rich flavors that have been passed down through generations. Each recipe in this chapter is a tribute to those sweet memories and the traditions that make Southern desserts so beloved. So, let's dive into these classic sweet treats that are sure to become your family's favorites.

| 128 | - SWEET TREATS

Peach Cobbler

Servings: 8 | *Prep Time:* 15 mins | *Cook Time:* 40 mins
Ingredients:

- 4 cups sliced fresh peaches (or canned, drained)
- 1 cup granulated sugar
- 1/2 cup butter, melted
- 1 cup all-purpose flour
- 1 cup granulated sugar
- 1 tablespoon baking powder
- 1/4 teaspoon salt
- 1 cup milk
- 1 teaspoon vanilla extract

Instructions:

1. Preheat oven to 375°F (190°C). Grease a 9x13-inch baking dish.
2. In a medium bowl, combine peaches and 1 cup sugar. Let sit for 10 minutes.
3. Pour melted butter into the prepared baking dish.
4. In a large bowl, whisk together flour, 1 cup sugar, baking powder, and salt. Stir in milk and vanilla extract until just combined.
5. Pour the batter over the melted butter in the baking dish. Do not stir.
6. Spoon the peaches and their juices evenly over the batter. Do not stir.

7. Bake for 35-40 minutes, or until the top is golden brown and the batter is set.
8. Serve warm, preferably with a scoop of vanilla ice cream.

Nutritional Information:

- Calories: 300
- Protein: 3g
- Carbs: 50g
- Fat: 10g

Cooking Tips:

- For extra flavor, add a pinch of cinnamon and nutmeg to the peaches.
- Use a mix of fresh and canned peaches for a more complex texture.

Allergen Information:

- Contains dairy and gluten. Use dairy-free butter and gluten-free flour if needed.

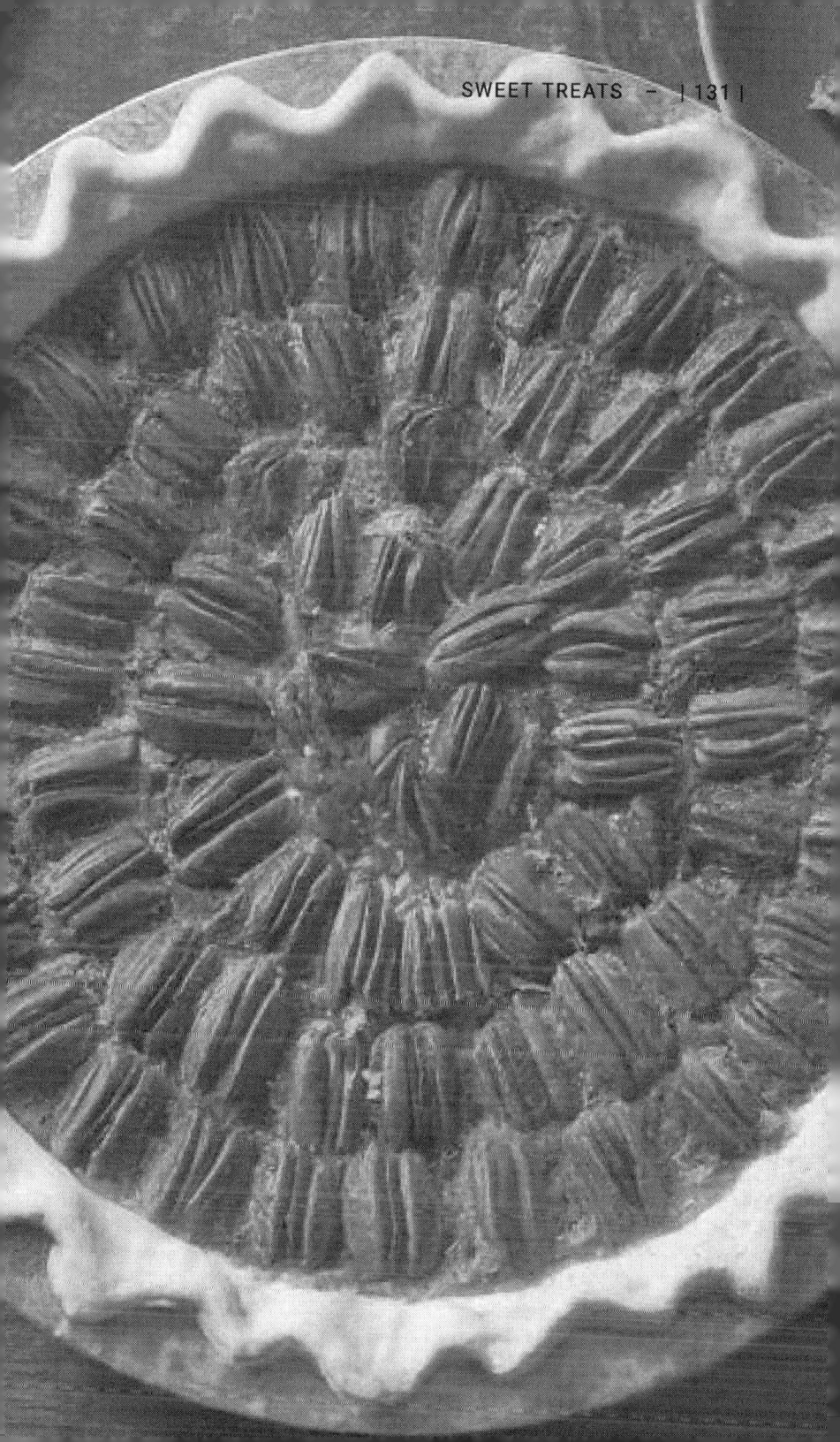

SWEET TREATS — |131|

Pecan Pie

Servings: 8 | *Prep Time:* 15 mins | *Cook Time:* 55 mins
Ingredients:

- 1 pie crust (store-bought or homemade)
- 1 cup light corn syrup
- 1 cup granulated sugar
- 1/2 cup butter, melted
- 3 large eggs, beaten
- 1 teaspoon vanilla extract
- 1 1/2 cups pecan halves

Instructions:

1. Preheat oven to 350°F (175°C). Place the pie crust in a 9-inch pie dish and set aside.
2. In a large bowl, combine corn syrup, sugar, melted butter, beaten eggs, and vanilla extract. Mix well.
3. Stir in pecan halves.
4. Pour the mixture into the pie crust.
5. Bake for 50-55 minutes, or until the pie is set and the top is golden brown.
6. Let cool completely before serving.

Nutritional Information:

- Calories: 500
- Protein: 5g
- Carbs: 65g

- Fat: 25g

Cooking Tips:

- For a richer flavor, use dark corn syrup instead of light.
- Serve with a dollop of whipped cream or a scoop of vanilla ice cream.

Allergen Information:

- Contains dairy, eggs, and nuts. Use dairy-free butter if needed.

| 134 | - SWEET TREATS

Red Velvet Cake

Servings: 12 | *Prep Time:* 20 mins | *Cook Time:* 30 mins
Ingredients:

- 2 1/2 cups all-purpose flour
- 1 1/2 cups granulated sugar
- 1 teaspoon baking soda
- 1 teaspoon salt
- 1 teaspoon cocoa powder
- 1 1/2 cups vegetable oil
- 1 cup buttermilk, room temperature
- 2 large eggs, room temperature
- 2 tablespoons red food coloring
- 1 teaspoon vanilla extract
- 1 teaspoon white vinegar
- 1/2 cup butter, softened
- 8 ounces cream cheese, softened
- 4 cups powdered sugar
- 1 teaspoon vanilla extract

Instructions:

1. Preheat oven to 350°F (175°C). Grease and flour two 9-inch round cake pans.
2. In a large bowl, sift together flour, sugar, baking soda, salt, and cocoa powder.
3. In another bowl, whisk together vegetable oil, buttermilk, eggs, red food coloring, vanilla extract, and vinegar.

4. Gradually add the dry ingredients to the wet ingredients, mixing until smooth.
5. Divide the batter evenly between the prepared cake pans.
6. Bake for 25-30 minutes, or until a toothpick inserted into the center comes out clean.
7. Let the cakes cool in the pans for 10 minutes, then transfer to wire racks to cool completely.
8. For the frosting, beat together butter and cream cheese until creamy. Gradually add powdered sugar and vanilla extract, beating until smooth.
9. Frost the cooled cakes and assemble.

Nutritional Information:

- Calories: 600
- Protein: 5g
- Carbs: 85g
- Fat: 25g

Cooking Tips:

- For a deeper red color, use gel food coloring instead of liquid.
- Add a teaspoon of espresso powder to the batter for a richer flavor.

Allergen Information:

- Contains dairy, eggs, and gluten. Use dairy-free butter and cream cheese, and gluten-free flour if needed.

SWEET TREATS — |137|

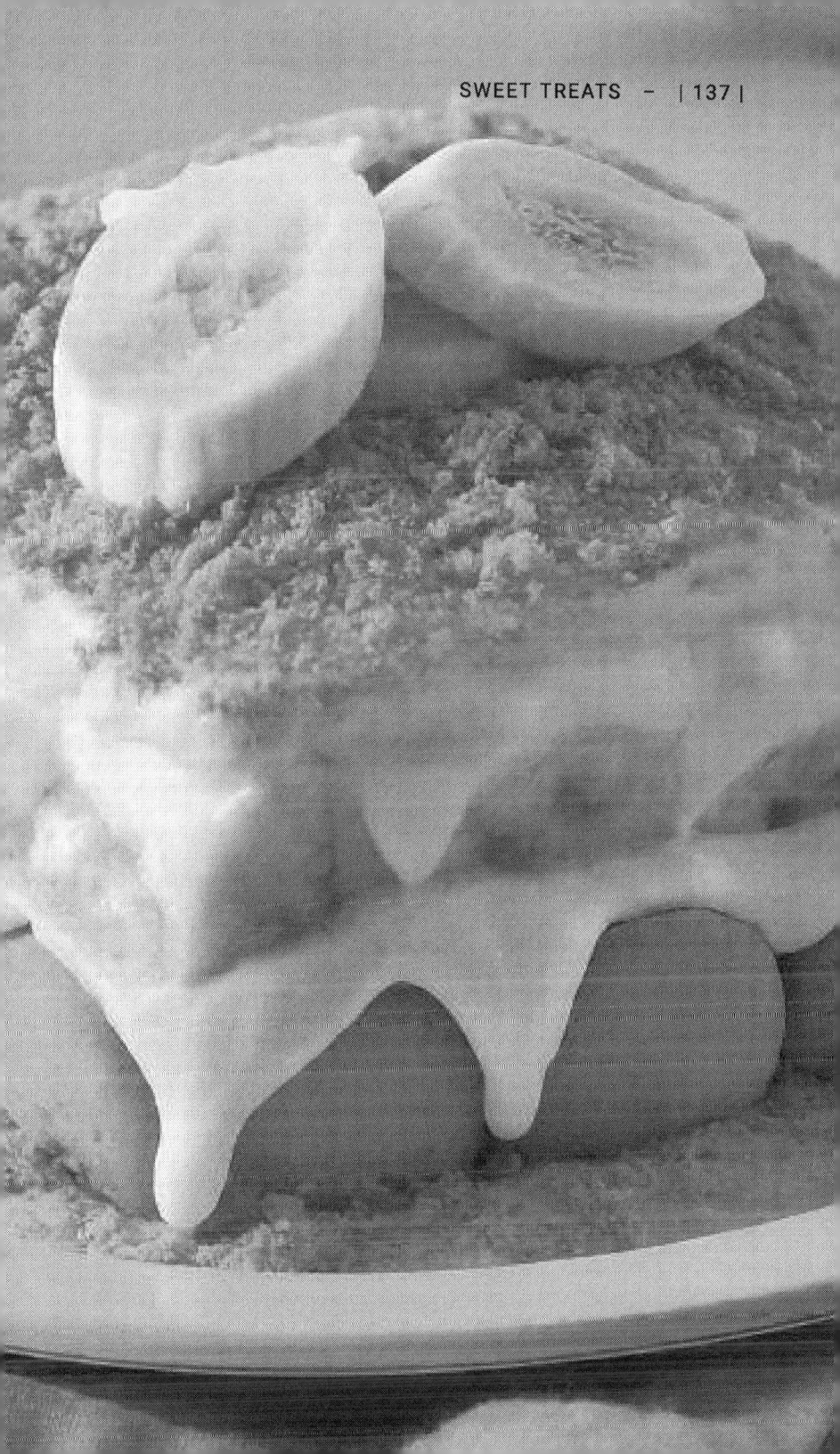

Banana Pudding

Servings: 8 | *Prep Time:* 20 mins | *Cook Time:* 10 mins
Ingredients:

- 3/4 cup granulated sugar
- 1/3 cup all-purpose flour
- 1/4 teaspoon salt
- 4 large egg yolks
- 2 cups milk
- 1/2 teaspoon vanilla extract
- 1 box vanilla wafers
- 4-5 ripe bananas, sliced
- 1 cup heavy cream
- 2 tablespoons powdered sugar
- 1/2 teaspoon vanilla extract

Instructions:

1. In a medium saucepan, whisk together sugar, flour, and salt. Add egg yolks and milk, whisking to combine.
2. Cook over medium heat, stirring constantly, until the mixture thickens and comes to a boil. Remove from heat and stir in vanilla extract.
3. In a 9x13-inch baking dish, layer vanilla wafers, banana slices, and pudding. Repeat layers until all ingredients are used.
4. In a large bowl, beat heavy cream, powdered sugar, and vanilla extract until stiff peaks form. Spread over the top of the pudding.
5. Refrigerate for at least 2 hours before serving.

Nutritional Information:

- Calories: 350
- Protein: 5g
- Carbs: 55g
- Fat: 15g

Cooking Tips:

- For extra flavor, toast the vanilla wafers before assembling the pudding.
- Add a splash of banana liqueur to the pudding mixture for a more intense banana flavor.

Allergen Information:

- Contains dairy, eggs, and gluten. Use dairy-free milk and cream, and gluten-free wafers if needed.

| 140 | - SWEET TREATS

Bread Pudding

Servings: 8 | *Prep Time:* 15 mins | *Cook Time:* 45 mins
Ingredients:

- 4 cups cubed bread (preferably day-old)
- 2 cups milk
- 1/2 cup granulated sugar
- 1/4 cup butter, melted
- 2 large eggs
- 1 teaspoon vanilla extract
- 1/2 teaspoon ground cinnamon
- 1/4 teaspoon ground nutmeg
- 1/2 cup raisins (optional)
- 1/2 cup brown sugar
- 1/4 cup butter
- 1/4 cup heavy cream
- 1/2 teaspoon vanilla extract

Instructions:

1. Preheat oven to 350°F (175°C). Grease a 9x13-inch baking dish.
2. In a large bowl, combine cubed bread and milk. Let soak for 10 minutes.
3. In another bowl, whisk together granulated sugar, melted butter, eggs, vanilla extract, cinnamon, and nutmeg. Stir in raisins, if using.
4. Pour the egg mixture over the soaked bread and stir to combine. Pour into the prepared baking dish.

5. Bake for 45-50 minutes, or until the top is golden brown and a toothpick inserted into the center comes out clean.
6. For the sauce, combine brown sugar, butter, and heavy cream in a small saucepan. Cook over medium heat until the mixture comes to a boil. Remove from heat and stir in vanilla extract.
7. Serve the bread pudding warm, drizzled with the sauce.

Nutritional Information:

- Calories: 400
- Protein: 7g
- Carbs: 55g
- Fat: 18g

Cooking Tips:

- Use a mix of different breads, such as brioche and French bread, for added texture.
- Add a handful of chopped nuts or chocolate chips for extra flavor.

Allergen Information:

- Contains dairy, eggs, and gluten. Use dairy-free milk and butter, and gluten-free bread if needed.

SWEET TREATS — | 143 |

Chocolate Chip Cookies

Servings: 24 | *Prep Time:* 15 mins | *Cook Time:* 10 mins

Ingredients:

- 2 1/4 cups all-purpose flour
- 1 teaspoon baking soda
- 1/2 teaspoon salt
- 1 cup unsalted butter, softened
- 3/4 cup granulated sugar
- 3/4 cup brown sugar
- 1 teaspoon vanilla extract
- 2 large eggs
- 2 cups semisweet chocolate chips

Instructions:

1. Preheat oven to 375°F (190°C). Line baking sheets with parchment paper.
2. In a medium bowl, whisk together flour, baking soda, and salt.
3. In a large bowl, beat together butter, granulated sugar, and brown sugar until creamy. Add vanilla extract and eggs, one at a time, beating well after each addition.
4. Gradually add the dry ingredients to the wet ingredients, mixing until just combined. Stir in chocolate chips.
5. Drop rounded tablespoons of dough onto the prepared baking sheets.
6. Bake for 9-11 minutes, or until the edges are golden brown. Cool on baking sheets for 2 minutes, then transfer to wire racks to cool completely.

Nutritional Information:

- Calories: 200
- Protein: 2g
- Carbs: 27g
- Fat: 10g

Cooking Tips:

- For chewier cookies, use melted butter and chill the dough before baking.
- Add a pinch of sea salt on top of the cookies before baking for a sweet and salty contrast.

Allergen Information:

- Contains dairy, eggs, and gluten. Use dairy-free butter and chocolate chips, and gluten-free flour if needed.

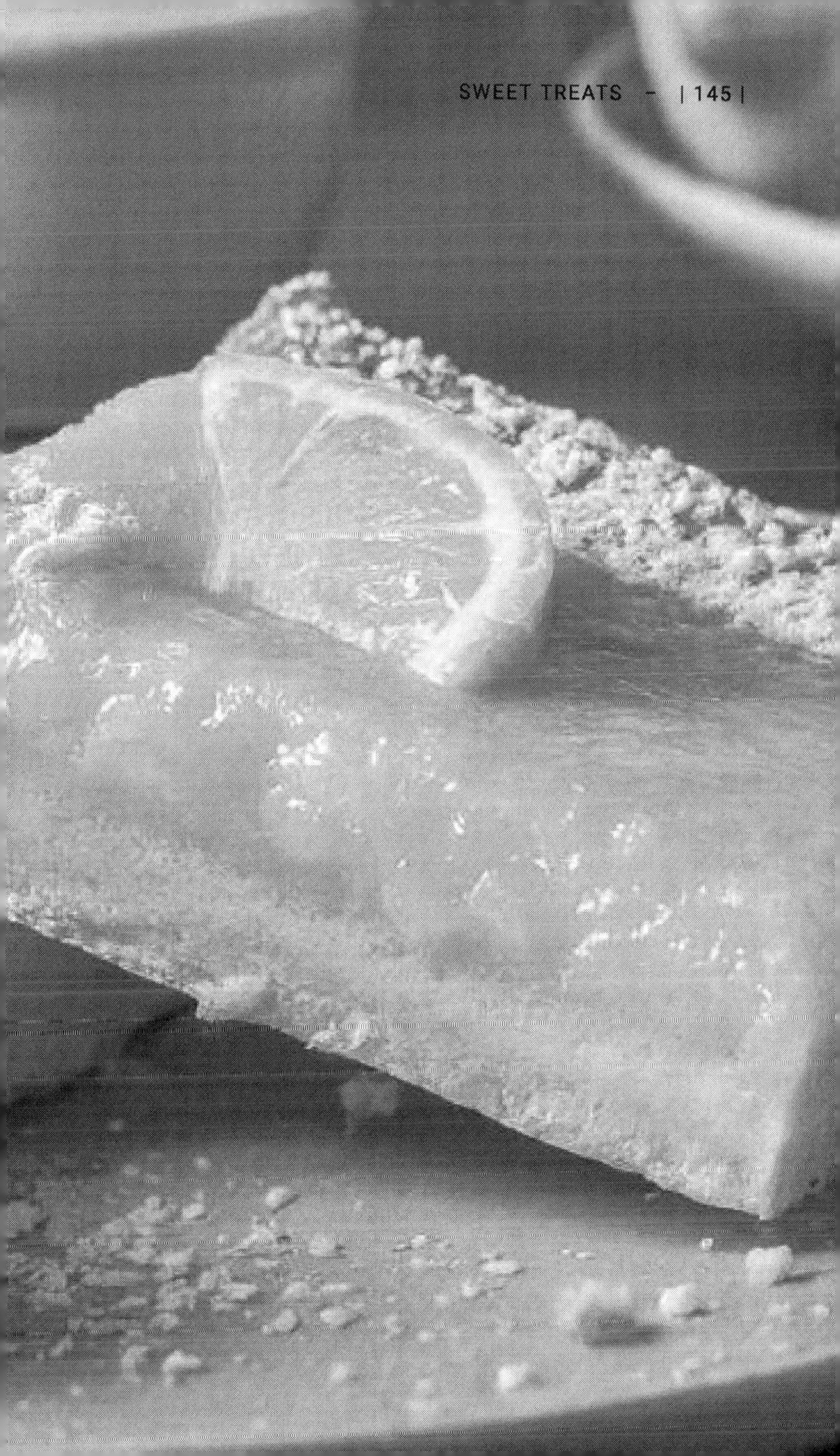

Lemon Bars

Servings: 16 | *Prep Time:* 15 mins | *Cook Time:* 35 mins
Ingredients:

- 1 cup all-purpose flour
- 1/4 cup granulated sugar
- 1/2 cup butter, softened
- 1 cup granulated sugar
- 2 large eggs
- 1/2 cup lemon juice
- 2 tablespoons all-purpose flour
- 1/2 teaspoon baking powder
- Powdered sugar, for dusting

Instructions:

1. Preheat oven to 350°F (175°C). Grease an 8x8-inch baking dish.
2. In a medium bowl, combine 1 cup flour, 1/4 cup granulated sugar, and softened butter. Press the mixture into the bottom of the prepared baking dish.
3. Bake for 15-20 minutes, or until the crust is golden brown.
4. In another bowl, whisk together 1 cup granulated sugar, eggs, lemon juice, 2 tablespoons flour, and baking powder until smooth.
5. Pour the lemon mixture over the hot crust.
6. Bake for 20-25 minutes, or until the filling is set and the top is lightly browned.

7. Let cool completely, then dust with powdered sugar before serving.

Nutritional Information:

- Calories: 150
- Protein: 2g
- Carbs: 22g
- Fat: 7g

Cooking Tips:

- For a more intense lemon flavor, add a teaspoon of lemon zest to the filling.
- Chill the bars in the refrigerator before cutting for cleaner slices.

Allergen Information:

- Contains dairy, eggs, and gluten. Use dairy-free butter and gluten-free flour if needed.

| 148 | - SWEET TREATS

Key Lime Pie

Servings: 8 | *Prep Time:* 20 mins | *Cook Time:* 15 mins
Ingredients:

- 1 1/2 cups graham cracker crumbs
- 1/4 cup granulated sugar
- 1/2 cup butter, melted
- 4 large egg yolks
- 1 can (14 ounces) sweetened condensed milk
- 1/2 cup key lime juice
- 1 teaspoon lime zest
- Whipped cream, for serving

Instructions:

1. Preheat oven to 350°F (175°C). Grease a 9-inch pie dish.
2. In a medium bowl, combine graham cracker crumbs, granulated sugar, and melted butter. Press the mixture into the bottom and up the sides of the prepared pie dish.
3. Bake for 8-10 minutes, or until the crust is lightly browned. Let cool completely.
4. In a large bowl, beat egg yolks until thick and pale. Gradually add sweetened condensed milk, key lime juice, and lime zest, beating until smooth.
5. Pour the filling into the cooled crust.
6. Bake for 15 minutes, or until the filling is set.
7. Let cool completely, then refrigerate for at least 2 hours before serving.
8. Serve with whipped cream.

Nutritional Information:

- Calories: 300
- Protein: 6g
- Carbs: 45g
- Fat: 12g

Cooking Tips:

- For a tarter pie, use more key lime juice.
- Garnish with lime slices or zest for a decorative touch.

Allergen Information:

- Contains dairy, eggs, and gluten. Use dairy-free butter and sweetened condensed milk, and gluten-free graham crackers if needed.

SWEET TREATS — | 151 |

Sweet Potato Pie

Servings: 8 | *Prep Time:* 20 mins | *Cook Time:* 55 mins
Ingredients:

- 1 pie crust (store-bought or homemade)
- 2 cups mashed sweet potatoes
- 1/2 cup brown sugar
- 1/2 cup granulated sugar
- 1/2 cup butter, melted
- 2 large eggs
- 1/2 cup milk
- 1 teaspoon vanilla extract
- 1/2 teaspoon ground cinnamon
- 1/4 teaspoon ground nutmeg
- Whipped cream, for serving

Instructions:

1. Preheat oven to 350°F (175°C). Place the pie crust in a 9-inch pie dish and set aside.
2. In a large bowl, combine mashed sweet potatoes, brown sugar, granulated sugar, melted butter, eggs, milk, vanilla extract, cinnamon, and nutmeg. Mix until smooth.
3. Pour the filling into the pie crust.
4. Bake for 50-55 minutes, or until the pie is set and the top is lightly browned.
5. Let cool completely before serving.
6. Serve with whipped cream.

Nutritional Information:

- Calories: 350
- Protein: 5g
- Carbs: 50g
- Fat: 15g

Cooking Tips:

- For a richer flavor, use evaporated milk instead of regular milk.
- Garnish with toasted pecans for added texture.

Allergen Information:

- Contains dairy, eggs, and gluten. Use dairy-free butter and milk, and gluten-free pie crust if needed.

SWEET TREATS

Caramel Cake

Servings: 12 | *Prep Time:* 20 mins | *Cook Time:* 30 mins
Ingredients:

- 2 1/2 cups all-purpose flour
- 2 cups granulated sugar
- 1 teaspoon baking powder
- 1/2 teaspoon baking soda
- 1/2 teaspoon salt
- 1 cup butter, softened
- 1 cup buttermilk, room temperature
- 4 large eggs, room temperature
- 2 teaspoons vanilla extract
- 1 cup brown sugar
- 1/2 cup butter
- 1/4 cup heavy cream
- 1 teaspoon vanilla extract
- 2 cups powdered sugar

Instructions:

1. Preheat oven to 350°F (175°C). Grease and flour two 9-inch round cake pans.
2. In a large bowl, whisk together flour, granulated sugar, baking powder, baking soda, and salt.
3. Add softened butter, buttermilk, eggs, and vanilla extract. Beat until smooth.
4. Divide the batter evenly between the prepared cake pans.

5. Bake for 25-30 minutes, or until a toothpick inserted into the center comes out clean.
6. Let the cakes cool in the pans for 10 minutes, then transfer to wire racks to cool completely.
7. For the frosting, combine brown sugar and butter in a saucepan. Cook over medium heat until the sugar is dissolved and the mixture is bubbly.
8. Remove from heat and stir in heavy cream and vanilla extract. Gradually add powdered sugar, beating until smooth.
9. Frost the cooled cakes and assemble.

Nutritional Information:

- Calories: 500
- Protein: 4g
- Carbs: 70g
- Fat: 22g

Cooking Tips:

- For a richer caramel flavor, cook the brown sugar and butter mixture longer until it darkens.
- Add a pinch of sea salt to the frosting for a salted caramel twist.

Allergen Information:

- Contains dairy, eggs, and gluten. Use dairy-free butter and buttermilk, and gluten-free flour if needed.

7

Snacks and Appetizers

In the South, snacking isn't just about grabbing a quick bite; it's an experience that brings people together. Whether it's a casual get-together, a lively party, or a family gathering, Southern appetizers and snacks set the stage for great conversations and lasting memories. These recipes are crafted to bring that spirit of hospitality to your table, offering a mix of crunchy, creamy, and savory delights that are sure to please any crowd. So, let's dive into these delectable snacks and appetizers that will make any occasion special.

| 158 | - SNACKS AND APPETIZERS

Fried Green Tomatoes

Servings: 6 | *Prep Time:* 15 mins | *Cook Time:* 15 mins
Ingredients:

- 4 large green tomatoes, sliced
- 1 cup buttermilk
- 1 cup cornmeal
- 1/2 cup all-purpose flour
- 1 teaspoon salt
- 1/2 teaspoon black pepper
- 1/2 teaspoon paprika
- Vegetable oil, for frying

Instructions:

1. In a large bowl, soak tomato slices in buttermilk for 10 minutes.
2. In another bowl, combine cornmeal, flour, salt, pepper, and paprika.
3. Heat vegetable oil in a large skillet over medium-high heat.
4. Remove tomato slices from buttermilk, letting excess drip off, and dredge in the cornmeal mixture, coating completely.
5. Fry the tomatoes in the hot oil until golden brown, about 3-4 minutes per side. Remove and drain on paper towels.
6. Serve hot with your favorite dipping sauce.

Nutritional Information:

- Calories: 200

- Protein: 4g
- Carbs: 30g
- Fat: 8g

Cooking Tips:

- For extra crispiness, double-dip the tomatoes in buttermilk and cornmeal.
- Serve with remoulade or ranch dressing for a flavorful dip.

Allergen Information:

- Contains gluten and dairy. Use gluten-free flour and a dairy-free buttermilk alternative if needed.

SNACKS AND APPETIZERS — | 161 |

Buffalo Wings

Servings: 4 | *Prep Time:* 10 mins | *Cook Time:* 25 mins
Ingredients:

- 2 pounds chicken wings
- 1/2 cup all-purpose flour
- 1/2 teaspoon salt
- 1/2 teaspoon black pepper
- 1/2 teaspoon paprika
- 1/2 cup hot sauce
- 1/4 cup butter, melted

Instructions:

1. Preheat oven to 400°F (200°C). Line a baking sheet with foil and place a wire rack on top.
2. In a large bowl, combine flour, salt, pepper, and paprika. Toss the chicken wings in the flour mixture until evenly coated.
3. Place the wings on the wire rack and bake for 20-25 minutes, or until golden and crispy.
4. In a small bowl, whisk together hot sauce and melted butter.
5. Toss the baked wings in the hot sauce mixture until well coated.
6. Serve hot with celery sticks and blue cheese dressing.

Nutritional Information:

- Calories: 350
- Protein: 25g

- Carbs: 5g
- Fat: 25g

Cooking Tips:

- For extra crispy wings, bake them at a higher temperature (450°F) for a shorter time (15-20 minutes).
- Adjust the amount of hot sauce to suit your heat preference.

Allergen Information:

- Gluten-free. Use gluten-free flour if needed.

SNACKS AND APPETIZERS

Spinach and Artichoke Dip

Servings: 8 | *Prep Time:* 10 mins | *Cook Time:* 20 mins
Ingredients:

- 1 (10-ounce) package frozen chopped spinach, thawed and drained
- 1 (14-ounce) can artichoke hearts, drained and chopped
- 1 cup mayonnaise
- 1 cup grated Parmesan cheese
- 1 cup shredded mozzarella cheese
- 1 teaspoon garlic powder
- 1/2 teaspoon black pepper

Instructions:

1. Preheat oven to 350°F (175°C). Grease a baking dish.
2. In a large bowl, combine spinach, artichoke hearts, mayonnaise, Parmesan cheese, mozzarella cheese, garlic powder, and black pepper. Mix until well combined.
3. Spread the mixture into the prepared baking dish.
4. Bake for 20-25 minutes, or until the top is golden and bubbly.
5. Serve hot with tortilla chips, crackers, or bread.

Nutritional Information:

- Calories: 250
- Protein: 10g
- Carbs: 5g
- Fat: 22g

Cooking Tips:

- For a creamier dip, add 1/2 cup of sour cream or cream cheese to the mixture.
- Garnish with chopped parsley or green onions for added color and flavor.

Allergen Information:

- Contains dairy and eggs. Use dairy-free cheese and mayonnaise if needed.

SNACKS AND APPETIZERS — |167|

Cheese Straws

Servings: 24 | *Prep Time:* 15 mins | *Cook Time:* 15 mins
Ingredients:

- 2 cups all-purpose flour
- 1/2 teaspoon salt
- 1/4 teaspoon cayenne pepper
- 1/2 cup cold butter, cubed
- 2 cups shredded sharp cheddar cheese
- 1/4 cup cold water

Instructions:

1. Preheat oven to 375°F (190°C). Line a baking sheet with parchment paper.
2. In a large bowl, combine flour, salt, and cayenne pepper. Cut in the cold butter until the mixture resembles coarse crumbs.
3. Stir in shredded cheddar cheese. Gradually add cold water, mixing until the dough comes together.
4. On a lightly floured surface, roll out the dough to 1/4-inch thickness. Cut into strips about 1/2-inch wide and 4 inches long.
5. Place the strips on the prepared baking sheet.
6. Bake for 12-15 minutes, or until golden and crispy. Let cool completely before serving.

Nutritional Information:

- Calories: 100

- Protein: 3g
- Carbs: 8g
- Fat: 7g

Cooking Tips:

- For a spicier version, add more cayenne pepper or a pinch of smoked paprika.
- Store in an airtight container to keep the cheese straws crispy.

Allergen Information:

- Contains dairy and gluten. Use gluten-free flour and dairy-free cheese if needed.

— SNACKS AND APPETIZERS

Mini Sausage Biscuits

Servings: 12 | *Prep Time:* 10 mins | *Cook Time:* 15 mins
Ingredients:

- 2 cups all-purpose flour
- 1 tablespoon baking powder
- 1/2 teaspoon salt
- 1/2 cup cold butter, cubed
- 3/4 cup milk
- 1/2 pound breakfast sausage, cooked and crumbled

Instructions:

1. Preheat oven to 425°F (220°C). Line a baking sheet with parchment paper.
2. In a large bowl, combine flour, baking powder, and salt. Cut in the cold butter until the mixture resembles coarse crumbs.
3. Stir in the milk until just combined. Fold in the cooked sausage.
4. On a lightly floured surface, roll out the dough to 1/2-inch thickness. Cut into small biscuits using a 2-inch round cutter.
5. Place the biscuits on the prepared baking sheet.
6. Bake for 12-15 minutes, or until golden brown.
7. Serve warm.

Nutritional Information:

- Calories: 150
- Protein: 4g

- Carbs: 15g
- Fat: 8g

Cooking Tips:

- For extra flavor, add shredded cheese to the dough.
- Serve with honey or jam for a sweet and savory combination.

Allergen Information:

- Contains dairy and gluten. Use gluten-free flour and dairy-free milk if needed.

SNACKS AND APPETIZERS — | 173 |

Stuffed Jalapenos

Servings: 12 | *Prep Time:* 15 mins | *Cook Time:* 15 mins
Ingredients:

- 12 large jalapenos, halved and seeded
- 8 ounces cream cheese, softened
- 1 cup shredded cheddar cheese
- 1/2 teaspoon garlic powder
- 1/2 teaspoon onion powder
- 12 slices bacon, cut in half

Instructions:

1. Preheat oven to 400°F (200°C). Line a baking sheet with parchment paper.
2. In a medium bowl, combine cream cheese, shredded cheddar cheese, garlic powder, and onion powder. Mix until well combined.
3. Fill each jalapeno half with the cheese mixture.
4. Wrap each stuffed jalapeno with a half slice of bacon and secure with a toothpick.
5. Place the stuffed jalapenos on the prepared baking sheet.
6. Bake for 15-20 minutes, or until the bacon is crispy and the cheese is melted.
7. Serve hot.

Nutritional Information:

- Calories: 200

- Protein: 7g
- Carbs: 3g
- Fat: 18g

Cooking Tips:

- For a spicier version, leave some of the seeds in the jalapenos.
- Serve with ranch dressing or sour cream for dipping.

Allergen Information:

- Contains dairy. Use dairy-free cream cheese and cheese if needed.

| 176 | - SNACKS AND APPETIZERS

Homemade Pickles

Servings: 24 | *Prep Time:* 10 mins | *Cook Time:* 0 mins (plus 24 hrs for marinating)

Ingredients:

- 6 cups cucumber slices
- 1 cup sliced onions
- 1 cup sliced bell peppers
- 2 cups white vinegar
- 2 cups water
- 1/4 cup salt
- 1/4 cup granulated sugar
- 1 tablespoon pickling spice
- 2 cloves garlic, minced

Instructions:

1. In a large bowl, combine cucumber slices, sliced onions, and sliced bell peppers.
2. In a medium saucepan, combine white vinegar, water, salt, sugar, pickling spice, and garlic. Bring to a boil, stirring until the salt and sugar are dissolved.
3. Pour the hot vinegar mixture over the vegetables. Let cool to room temperature.
4. Transfer the mixture to jars and refrigerate for at least 24 hours before serving.

Nutritional Information:

- Calories: 10
- Protein: 0g
- Carbs: 2g
- Fat: 0g

Cooking Tips:

- For sweeter pickles, increase the amount of sugar.
- Add red pepper flakes for a spicy kick.

Allergen Information:

- Gluten-free and dairy-free.

SNACKS AND APPETIZERS — | 179 |

Pimento Cheese Balls

Servings: 24 | *Prep Time:* 10 mins | *Cook Time:* 0 mins
Ingredients:

- 2 cups shredded sharp cheddar cheese
- 1/2 cup mayonnaise
- 1 (4-ounce) jar diced pimentos, drained
- 1/4 teaspoon garlic powder
- 1/4 teaspoon onion powder
- 1/4 teaspoon cayenne pepper
- 1 cup finely chopped pecans

Instructions:

1. In a large bowl, combine shredded cheddar cheese, mayonnaise, diced pimentos, garlic powder, onion powder, and cayenne pepper. Mix until well combined.
2. Roll the mixture into small balls.
3. Roll each ball in chopped pecans to coat.
4. Chill in the refrigerator for at least 1 hour before serving.

Nutritional Information:

- Calories: 100
- Protein: 3g
- Carbs: 2g
- Fat: 9g

Cooking Tips:

- For a smoother texture, blend the mixture in a food processor before rolling into balls.
- Serve with crackers or bread.

Allergen Information:

- Contains dairy and nuts. Use dairy-free cheese and mayonnaise, and omit nuts if needed.

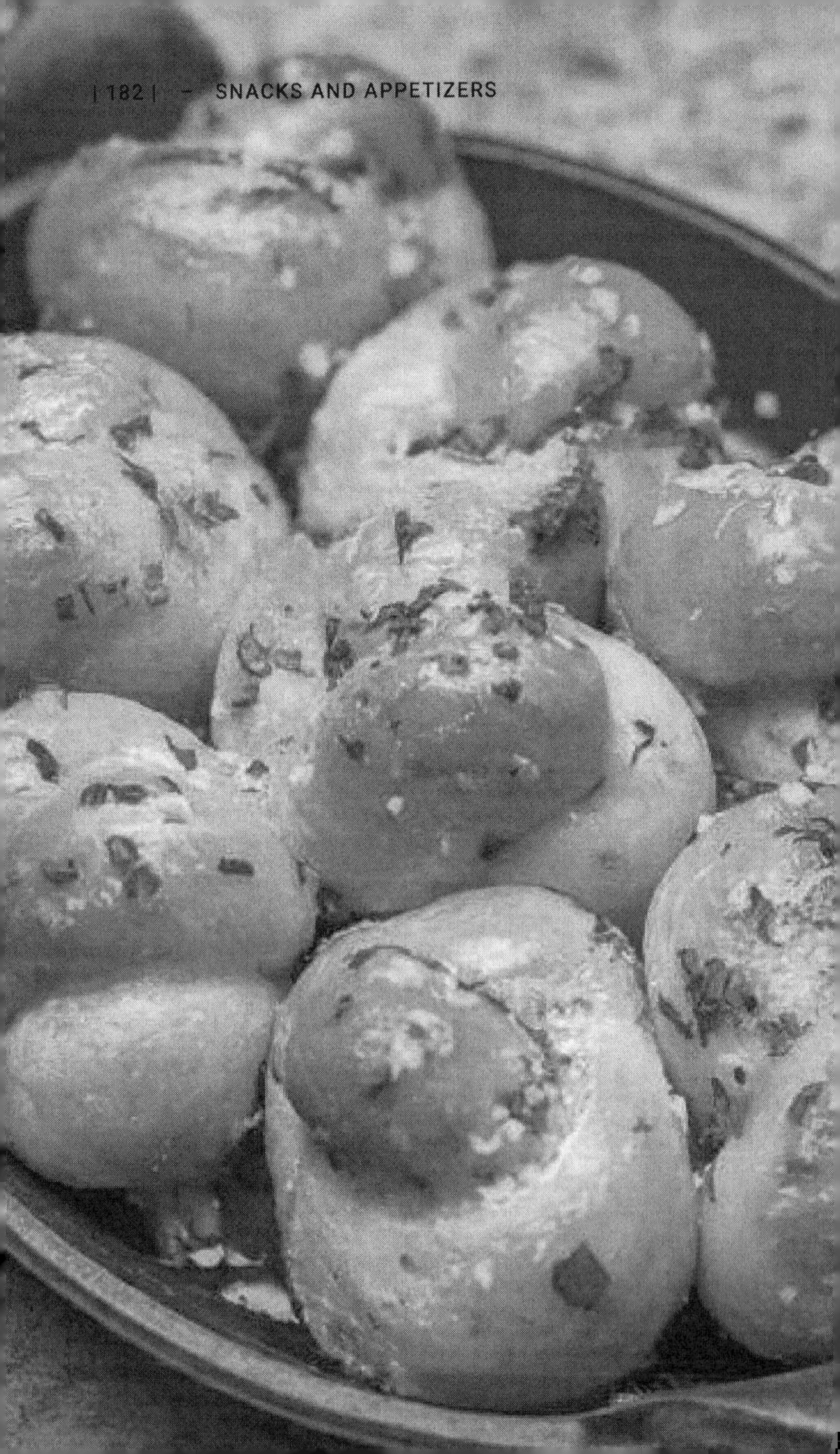

Garlic Knots

Servings: 24 | *Prep Time:* 10 mins | *Cook Time:* 15 mins
Ingredients:

- 1 pound pizza dough
- 4 tablespoons butter, melted
- 4 cloves garlic, minced
- 1/4 cup grated Parmesan cheese
- 1 tablespoon chopped fresh parsley
- Salt and pepper to taste

Instructions:

1. Preheat oven to 375°F (190°C). Line a baking sheet with parchment paper.
2. On a lightly floured surface, roll out the pizza dough to 1/4-inch thickness. Cut into strips about 1 inch wide and 6 inches long.
3. Tie each strip into a knot and place on the prepared baking sheet.
4. In a small bowl, combine melted butter, minced garlic, Parmesan cheese, parsley, salt, and pepper. Brush the mixture over the knots.
5. Bake for 12-15 minutes, or until golden brown.
6. Serve warm.

Nutritional Information:

- Calories: 100

- Protein: 3g
- Carbs: 15g
- Fat: 3g

Cooking Tips:

- For extra flavor, sprinkle additional Parmesan cheese on top before baking.
- Serve with marinara sauce for dipping.

Allergen Information:

- Contains dairy and gluten. Use dairy-free butter and cheese, and gluten-free pizza dough if needed.

SNACKS AND APPETIZERS — |185|

Southern Crab Cakes

Servings: 6 | *Prep Time:* 15 mins | *Cook Time:* 15 mins
Ingredients:

- 1 pound lump crabmeat, picked over for shells
- 1/2 cup mayonnaise
- 1/4 cup finely chopped red bell pepper
- 1/4 cup finely chopped green onion
- 1 tablespoon Dijon mustard
- 1 tablespoon Worcestershire sauce
- 1 teaspoon Old Bay seasoning
- 1/2 teaspoon salt
- 1/2 teaspoon black pepper
- 1 cup bread crumbs
- 2 large eggs, beaten
- 2 tablespoons vegetable oil, for frying

Instructions:

1. In a large bowl, combine crabmeat, mayonnaise, red bell pepper, green onion, Dijon mustard, Worcestershire sauce, Old Bay seasoning, salt, black pepper, bread crumbs, and beaten eggs. Mix until well combined.
2. Shape the mixture into 6 patties.
3. Heat vegetable oil in a large skillet over medium-high heat. Fry the crab cakes until golden brown, about 3-4 minutes per side. Remove and drain on paper towels.
4. Serve hot with lemon wedges and tartar sauce.

Nutritional Information:

- Calories: 200
- Protein: 15g
- Carbs: 10g
- Fat: 10g

Cooking Tips:

- For extra flavor, add a splash of hot sauce to the crab mixture.
- Serve on a bed of mixed greens for a light meal.

Allergen Information:

- Contains gluten, dairy, and shellfish. Use gluten-free bread crumbs and dairy-free mayonnaise if needed.

8

Refreshing Beverages

No Southern gathering is complete without a refreshing beverage to sip on. Whether it's a tall glass of sweet tea on a hot day or a warm mug of apple cider on a cool evening, drinks play a vital role in Southern hospitality. These beverages are crafted to quench your thirst and bring a bit of Southern charm to any occasion. So, let's dive into these refreshing drinks that will keep you cool and satisfied all year round.

| 190 | - REFRESHING BEVERAGES

Sweet Tea

Servings: 8 | *Prep Time:* 10 mins | *Cook Time:* 5 mins
Ingredients:

- 8 cups water
- 6 black tea bags
- 1 cup granulated sugar
- 1/4 teaspoon baking soda
- Ice
- Lemon slices, for serving

Instructions:

1. In a large pot, bring 4 cups of water to a boil. Remove from heat and add tea bags. Steep for 5 minutes.
2. Remove tea bags and stir in sugar and baking soda until dissolved.
3. Add remaining 4 cups of water and stir to combine.
4. Let the tea cool to room temperature, then refrigerate until cold.
5. Serve over ice with lemon slices.

Nutritional Information:

- Calories: 100
- Protein: 0g
- Carbs: 25g
- Fat: 0g

Cooking Tips:

- For a less sweet version, reduce the amount of sugar.
- Add a sprig of fresh mint for a refreshing twist.

Allergen Information:

- Gluten-free and dairy-free.

REFRESHING BEVERAGES — | 193 |

Lemonade

Servings: 8 | *Prep Time:* 10 mins | *Cook Time:* 0 mins
Ingredients:

- 1 cup fresh lemon juice (about 6 lemons)
- 1 cup granulated sugar
- 8 cups water
- Ice
- Lemon slices and mint leaves, for serving

Instructions:

1. In a large pitcher, combine lemon juice and sugar. Stir until the sugar is dissolved.
2. Add water and stir to combine.
3. Serve over ice with lemon slices and mint leaves.

Nutritional Information:

- Calories: 80
- Protein: 0g
- Carbs: 21g
- Fat: 0g

Cooking Tips:

- For a sweeter lemonade, increase the amount of sugar.
- Add a splash of sparkling water for a fizzy version.

Allergen Information:

- Gluten-free and dairy-free.

| 196 | – REFRESHING BEVERAGES

Mint Julep

Servings: 1 | *Prep Time:* 5 mins | *Cook Time:* 0 mins
Ingredients:

- 8 fresh mint leaves, plus extra for garnish
- 1 tablespoon simple syrup
- 2 ounces bourbon
- Crushed ice
- Mint sprig, for garnish

Instructions:

1. In a julep cup or glass, muddle the mint leaves with simple syrup.
2. Add bourbon and fill the cup with crushed ice.
3. Stir until the cup is frosty.
4. Garnish with a mint sprig and serve immediately.

Nutritional Information:

- Calories: 150
- Protein: 0g
- Carbs: 10g
- Fat: 0g

Cooking Tips:

- For a non-alcoholic version, substitute bourbon with ginger ale.

- Use fresh, high-quality mint for the best flavor.

Allergen Information:

- Gluten-free and dairy-free.

REFRESHING BEVERAGES — |199|

Southern Punch

Servings: 12 | *Prep Time:* 10 mins | *Cook Time:* 0 mins
Ingredients:

- 4 cups pineapple juice
- 4 cups orange juice
- 2 cups cranberry juice
- 2 cups ginger ale
- Ice
- Orange slices and maraschino cherries, for garnish

Instructions:

1. In a large pitcher or punch bowl, combine pineapple juice, orange juice, cranberry juice, and ginger ale. Stir to combine.
2. Serve over ice, garnished with orange slices and maraschino cherries.

Nutritional Information:

- Calories: 110
- Protein: 0g
- Carbs: 27g
- Fat: 0g

Cooking Tips:

- For a more tropical flavor, add a splash of coconut water.
- Substitute ginger ale with sparkling water for a lighter punch.

Allergen Information:

- Gluten-free and dairy-free.

| 202 | - REFRESHING BEVERAGES

Peach Iced Tea

Servings: 8 | *Prep Time:* 10 mins | *Cook Time:* 10 mins
Ingredients:

- 8 cups water
- 4 black tea bags
- 2 cups peach nectar
- 1/2 cup granulated sugar
- Ice
- Peach slices and mint leaves, for serving

Instructions:

1. In a large pot, bring water to a boil. Remove from heat and add tea bags. Steep for 5 minutes.
2. Remove tea bags and stir in peach nectar and sugar until dissolved.
3. Let the tea cool to room temperature, then refrigerate until cold.
4. Serve over ice with peach slices and mint leaves.

Nutritional Information:

- Calories: 90
- Protein: 0g
- Carbs: 23g
- Fat: 0g

Cooking Tips:

- For a stronger peach flavor, add sliced peaches to the tea while it cools.
- Adjust the sweetness by adding more or less sugar to taste.

Allergen Information:

- Gluten-free and dairy-free.

REFRESHING BEVERAGES — | 205 |

Hot Apple Cider

Servings: 8 | *Prep Time:* 5 mins | *Cook Time:* 15 mins
Ingredients:

- 8 cups apple cider
- 1/4 cup brown sugar
- 1 teaspoon whole cloves
- 1 teaspoon whole allspice
- 3 cinnamon sticks
- Orange slices, for garnish

Instructions:

1. In a large pot, combine apple cider, brown sugar, cloves, allspice, and cinnamon sticks. Bring to a simmer over medium heat.
2. Simmer for 10-15 minutes, stirring occasionally.
3. Remove from heat and strain to remove spices.
4. Serve hot, garnished with orange slices.

Nutritional Information:

- Calories: 100
- Protein: 0g
- Carbs: 25g
- Fat: 0g

Cooking Tips:

- For a spiked version, add a splash of rum or bourbon.
- Garnish with a cinnamon stick for extra flavor and presentation.

Allergen Information:

- Gluten-free and dairy-free.

– REFRESHING BEVERAGES

Homemade Eggnog

Servings: 8 | *Prep Time:* 10 mins | *Cook Time:* 10 mins
Ingredients:

- 4 cups whole milk
- 1 cup heavy cream
- 5 large eggs
- 3/4 cup granulated sugar
- 1/2 cup bourbon or rum (optional)
- 1 teaspoon vanilla extract
- 1/2 teaspoon ground nutmeg
- Whipped cream and ground nutmeg, for serving

Instructions:

1. In a large saucepan, combine milk and heavy cream. Heat over medium heat until just simmering.
2. In a large bowl, whisk together eggs and sugar until well combined.
3. Slowly add the hot milk mixture to the eggs, whisking constantly.
4. Return the mixture to the saucepan and cook over low heat, stirring constantly, until the mixture thickens slightly and coats the back of a spoon.
5. Remove from heat and stir in bourbon or rum (if using), vanilla extract, and ground nutmeg.
6. Let cool to room temperature, then refrigerate until cold.
7. Serve topped with whipped cream and a sprinkle of ground nutmeg.

Nutritional Information:

- Calories: 250
- Protein: 6g
- Carbs: 20g
- Fat: 15g

Cooking Tips:

- For a non-alcoholic version, omit the bourbon or rum.
- Add a pinch of ground cinnamon for extra warmth and flavor.

Allergen Information:

- Contains dairy and eggs. Use dairy-free milk and cream, and an egg substitute if needed.

REFRESHING BEVERAGES — |211|

Blackberry Lemonade

Servings: 8 | *Prep Time:* 10 mins | *Cook Time:* 10 mins
Ingredients:

- 1 cup fresh blackberries
- 1 cup granulated sugar
- 1 cup fresh lemon juice (about 6 lemons)
- 8 cups water
- Ice
- Lemon slices and blackberries, for garnish

Instructions:

1. In a small saucepan, combine blackberries, sugar, and 1 cup of water. Bring to a boil, then reduce heat and simmer for 5 minutes, until the blackberries are soft and the sugar is dissolved.
2. Strain the blackberry mixture through a fine-mesh sieve into a large pitcher, pressing down on the solids to extract as much liquid as possible.
3. Add lemon juice and remaining 7 cups of water to the pitcher. Stir to combine.
4. Serve over ice, garnished with lemon slices and blackberries.

Nutritional Information:

- Calories: 80
- Protein: 0g
- Carbs: 21g
- Fat: 0g

Cooking Tips:

- For a fizzy version, substitute 2 cups of water with sparkling water.
- Adjust the sweetness by adding more or less sugar to taste.

Allergen Information:

- Gluten-free and dairy-free.

| 214 | – REFRESHING BEVERAGES

Arnold Palmer

Servings: 8 | *Prep Time:* 10 mins | *Cook Time:* 10 mins
Ingredients:

- 4 cups water
- 4 black tea bags
- 1 cup granulated sugar
- 1 cup fresh lemon juice (about 6 lemons)
- 4 cups cold water
- Ice
- Lemon slices, for garnish

Instructions:

1. In a medium saucepan, bring 4 cups of water to a boil. Remove from heat and add tea bags. Steep for 5 minutes.
2. Remove tea bags and stir in sugar until dissolved. Let cool to room temperature.
3. In a large pitcher, combine the sweetened tea, lemon juice, and cold water. Stir to combine.
4. Serve over ice, garnished with lemon slices.

Nutritional Information:

- Calories: 60
- Protein: 0g
- Carbs: 16g
- Fat: 0g

Cooking Tips:

- For a less sweet version, reduce the amount of sugar.
- Add fresh mint leaves for a refreshing twist.

Allergen Information:

- Gluten-free and dairy-free.

9

Cooking Tips and Techniques

Essential Kitchen Tools

Having the right tools in your kitchen can make all the difference in your cooking experience. Here are some must-have tools and gadgets that will help you prepare these Southern recipes with ease:

1. **Cast-Iron Skillet**: Perfect for frying, baking, and everything in between, a cast-iron skillet is durable and versatile.
2. **Dutch Oven**: Ideal for slow-cooking, braising, and making soups and stews.
3. **Mixing Bowls**: A variety of sizes for mixing, marinating, and preparing ingredients.
4. **Measuring Cups and Spoons**: Accurate measurements are crucial for baking and cooking.
5. **Chef's Knife**: A sharp, high-quality knife makes chopping and slicing safer and more efficient.
6. **Cutting Board**: A sturdy cutting board protects your countertops and makes food prep easier.
7. **Whisk**: Essential for mixing batters, sauces, and eggs.

8. **Baking Sheets and Pans**: Necessary for baking cookies, cakes, biscuits, and more.
9. **Stand Mixer or Hand Mixer**: Makes mixing doughs and batters much easier.
10. **Blender or Food Processor**: Useful for making sauces, purees, and chopping ingredients quickly.
11. **Thermometer**: Ensures your meats are cooked to the perfect temperature.

Cooking Basics

Mastering some fundamental cooking techniques will help you create delicious dishes with confidence. Here are a few key techniques to get you started:

1. **Sautéing**: Cooking food quickly in a small amount of oil over high heat. This technique is perfect for vegetables, meats, and aromatics like garlic and onions.

    ◦ Tip: Preheat your pan before adding oil and ingredients to prevent sticking and ensure even cooking.

2. **Braising**: Slow-cooking meat or vegetables in a small amount of liquid. Ideal for tougher cuts of meat that become tender and flavorful with time.

- Tip: Brown your meat first to develop a rich, deep flavor before adding your liquid and simmering.

3. **Baking**: Cooking food with dry heat in an oven. Perfect for cakes, cookies, bread, and casseroles.

    - Tip: Always preheat your oven and use the middle rack for even baking.

4. **Frying**: Cooking food in hot oil, either shallow frying or deep frying. Great for achieving a crispy, golden exterior.

    - Tip: Use a thermometer to maintain the correct oil temperature and avoid overcrowding the pan.

5. **Grilling**: Cooking food over direct heat, usually on a barbecue grill. Ideal for meats, vegetables, and even fruits.

    - Tip: Preheat your grill and oil the grates to prevent sticking.

6. **Roasting**: Cooking food in an oven with dry heat, typically at higher temperatures. Perfect for meats and vegetables.

- Tip: Toss vegetables in oil and seasonings before roasting for the best flavor.

7. **Simmering**: Cooking food gently in liquid at a low temperature. Ideal for soups, stews, and sauces.

    - Tip: Keep an eye on the heat and adjust to maintain a gentle simmer without boiling.

Ingredient Substitutions

Sometimes you might not have a particular ingredient on hand or need to accommodate dietary restrictions. Here are some common ingredient swaps and alternatives:

1. **Buttermilk**: Substitute with 1 cup of milk mixed with 1 tablespoon of lemon juice or vinegar. Let it sit for 5 minutes before using.
2. **Heavy Cream**: Use an equal amount of evaporated milk or a mixture of milk and melted butter (3/4 cup milk + 1/4 cup melted butter).
3. **Eggs**: For baking, replace each egg with 1/4 cup unsweetened applesauce, 1/4 cup mashed banana, or 1 tablespoon ground flaxseed mixed with 3 tablespoons water.
4. **All-Purpose Flour**: Substitute with a gluten-free flour blend in a 1:1 ratio.
5. **Sugar**: Use honey, maple syrup, or agave nectar in a 1:1 ratio, but reduce other liquid ingredients slightly.

6. **Butter**: Substitute with an equal amount of margarine, shortening, or coconut oil.
7. **Bread Crumbs**: Use crushed crackers, oats, or crushed cornflakes as a substitute.
8. **Mayonnaise**: Use Greek yogurt or sour cream for a lighter alternative.
9. **Soy Sauce**: Substitute with tamari or coconut aminos for a gluten-free option.
10. **Chicken Broth**: Use vegetable broth or water with a bit of salt and seasoning.

These tips and techniques will help you navigate through the recipes with ease, ensuring delicious results every time. Happy cooking!

Lila Thompson

Lila Thompson is a proud Southern cook who has spent her life savoring and sharing the rich culinary traditions of her heritage. Raised in a small town in Georgia, Lila grew up in a kitchen filled with the comforting aromas of home-cooked meals prepared by her mother and grandmother. From an early age, she learned that food is more than just sustenance; it's a way to bring people together, celebrate life's moments, and preserve cherished memories.

Lila's culinary journey began in her family's kitchen, where she watched and learned the secrets of Southern cooking from her grandmother's deft hands. Over the years, she honed her skills and developed her own unique style, blending traditional recipes with her own creative flair. Her passion for cooking led her to pursue a degree in culinary arts, where she further refined her techniques and expanded her repertoire.

After years of working in various restaurants and kitchens, Lila decided to return to her roots and focus on sharing the flavors and stories of Southern cuisine with a wider audience. She started a popular food blog, "Barefoot Neighbor Kitchen," where she shares her favorite recipes, cooking tips, and the stories behind the dishes. Her warm, engaging writing style and delicious recipes quickly garnered a loyal following, leading to the creation of this cookbook.

In "Y'all Come Fix You a Plate Cookbook," Lila brings together over 70 of her favorite recipes, each one infused with the love and warmth of her Southern upbringing. From hearty breakfasts to refreshing beverages, every recipe is crafted to make you feel like you're sitting at her kitchen table, enjoying a meal with family and friends.

When she's not in the kitchen, Lila enjoys tending to her garden, exploring local farmers' markets, and spending time with her family and friends. She believes that the best meals are those made with fresh, simple ingredients and shared with loved ones. Through this cookbook, Lila hopes to inspire home cooks everywhere to embrace the joy of Southern cooking and create their own culinary traditions.

Lila Thompson's journey from her grandmother's kitchen to becoming a beloved Southern cook and food blogger is a testament to her passion for food and family. Her recipes and stories are a celebration of Southern hospitality, and she invites you to join her in creating delicious meals that bring people together. Enjoy the flavors, the warmth, and the love that each recipe in this cookbook offers.

APPENDIX

Conversion Charts

Measurement	Equivalent
1 tablespoon (tbsp)	3 teaspoons (tsp)
1 cup	16 tablespoons (tbsp)
1 pint	2 cups
1 quart	4 cups
1 gallon	4 quarts
1 ounce (oz)	2 tablespoons (tbsp)
1 pound (lb)	16 ounces (oz)
1 milliliter (ml)	0.034 ounces (oz)
1 liter (L)	1.057 quarts
1 gram (g)	0.035 ounces (oz)
1 kilogram (kg)	2.205 pounds (lb)
1 inch (in)	2.54 centimeters (cm)
1 centimeter (cm)	0.3937 inches (in)

Glossary

Term	Explanation
Al dente	Pasta or rice that is cooked to be firm to the bite.
Braise	To cook meat or vegetables slowly in a small amount of liquid in a covered pot.
Broil	To cook food directly under or above a heat source.
Caramelize	To cook sugar until it turns brown and develops a rich flavor.
Chiffonade	A chopping technique in which herbs or leafy green vegetables are cut into long, thin strips.
Deglaze	To add liquid to a hot pan to loosen and dissolve food particles stuck to the bottom.
Dredge	To lightly coat food in flour or breadcrumbs before frying or sautéing.
Fold	To gently combine ingredients without knocking air out of the mixture.
Julienne	To cut vegetables into thin, matchstick-sized strips.

Term	Explanation
Knead	To work dough by hand or with a mixer to develop gluten and elasticity.
Macerate	To soak fruit in liquid (often sugar or alcohol) to soften and flavor it.
Mince	To cut food into very small pieces.
Poach	To cook food gently in simmering liquid just below boiling.
Purée	To blend food into a smooth, thick consistency.
Reduce	To cook a liquid until its volume decreases and its flavor intensifies.
Roux	A mixture of fat and flour cooked together and used to thicken sauces.
Sauté	To cook food quickly in a small amount of oil or butter over high heat.
Simmer	To cook food gently in liquid at a temperature just below boiling.
Steam	To cook food over boiling water without direct contact with the water.

Term	Explanation
Zest	The outer, colored skin of citrus fruit used for flavoring.

This appendix serves as a handy reference for measurement conversions and cooking terms to help you navigate recipes and techniques with ease.

Made in the USA
Columbia, SC
23 December 2024